D1191479

Religion in China

Major World Religions Series

Donald K. Swearer, Editor

Religion in China

BY RICHARD C. BUSH, Ph.D

52362

Argus Communications
Niles, Illinois 60648

ACKNOWLEDGMENTS

Excerpts from *Buddhism in China: A Historical Survey* by Kenneth S. Ch'en. Copyright © 1964 by Princeton University Press; Princeton paperback, 1972. Reprinted by permission of Princeton University Press.

The I Ching or Book of Changes. The Richard Wilhelm Translation rendered into English by Cary F. Baynes. 3d ed. Bollingen Series XIX. © 1950, 1967 by Bollingen Foundation. Excerpts from pp. 48–52 reprinted by permission of Princeton University Press, publisher of the Bollingen Series, and Routledge & Kegan Paul, London.

Excerpts from *A Source Book in Chinese Philosophy*, transl. and compiled by Wing-tsit Chan. Copyright © 1963 by Princeton University Press; Princeton paperback, 1969. Reprinted by permission of Princeton University Press.

Excerpts from *Sources of Chinese Tradition*, compiled by Wm. Theodore de Bary et al. New York: Columbia University Press, 1960. Reprinted by permission of Columbia University Press.

Excerpt from *The Wisdom of Confucius*, ed. and transl. by Lin Yutang. Copyright 1938 by The Modern Library. Reprinted by permission of Random House, Inc.

PHOTO CREDITS

Richard C. Bush vi, 4, 20, 24, 37, 40, 48, 61, 64, 73
Jean-Claude LeJeune cover: center, lower left, upper right
Gary Stallings/TOM STACK & ASSOCIATES cover: upper left, lower right

MAP

Homer Grooman

COVER DESIGN

Gene Tarpey

Argus Communications
7440 Natchez Avenue
Niles, Illinois 60648

International Standard Book Number 0–913592–98–6

Library of Congress Number 77–82796

1 2 3 4 5 6 7 8 9 0

Contents

Foreword

"The study of religion is the study of mankind." Religion touches the deepest feelings of the human heart and is part of every human society. In modern times religion has been studied by sociologists and anthropologists as a cultural institution. Psychologists see religion as an expression of an inner human need. Philosophers view it as a system of thought or doctrine. Historians consider religion a part of the intellectual and institutional development of a given era.

What is religion? Modern definitions range from "what man does in his solitude" to "an expression of collective identity," and from "man's experience of awe and fascination before a tremendous mystery" to "projective feelings of dependency." The scope of life that religion is identified with is so vast, and the assumptions about the nature of religion are so varied, that we may readily agree with those who say that the study of religion is the study of mankind.

Religion takes many forms, or perhaps it would be better to say that there are many aspects to religion. They include *belief* (e.g., the belief in a creator God), *ritual action* (e.g., making offerings to that God), *ethical action* (following God's law), the formation of *religious communities,* and the formulation of *creeds and doctrinal systems.*

Joachim Wach, a scholar of religion, has pictured religion in terms of religious experience which expresses itself in thought, action, and fellowship.[1] In this view religion is rooted in religious experience, and all other aspects of religion are expressions of that experience. For example, the Buddha's experience of the highest Truth (in Buddhism called *Nirvana*) led him to teach what he had experienced (known as *dharma*) and resulted in the formation of a monastic community (known as *sangha*).

It must be remembered that religions develop within particular historical and cultural traditions and not in a vacuum. This fact has several profound consequences for the study of religion. In the first place it means that religion can never be completely separated from particular historical and cultural traditions. For example, early

[1]Joachim Wach, *The Comparative Study of Religions* (New York: Columbia University Press, 1958).

Christian thought was deeply influenced by both Semitic and Greek traditions, and such central Christian celebrations as Christmas and Easter owe their form to pre-Christian European traditions.

Furthermore, since a religion is subject to cultural and historical influences, its traditions are always developing relative to particular times and places. For example, the form of worship used in the Buddhist Churches of America (founded in the late nineteenth century) has as much or more in common with American Protestant worship services than with its traditional Japanese form. A religion, then, as part of a specific historical and cultural stream, changes through time and can be fully understood only in relationship to its historical and cultural forms. By way of generalization we might say that Christianity as a religion is only partially understood in terms of its central beliefs and that a fuller or more complete understanding demands a knowledge of its worldwide history and the influence of its various cultural traditions.

In the second place, since a religion develops within particular historical and cultural settings, it also influences its setting. In other words, there is a give-and-take relationship between a religion and its environment. For example, in traditional societies like medieval Europe, Christianity was the inspiration for much of the art and architecture. The same is true for traditional India, where Buddhism and Hinduism decisively affected artistic forms, or for traditional Persia with Islam. Of course, religion influences its environment in other than merely artistic realms. It has had profound effects on modes of behavior (ethics), conceptions of state (politics), forms of economic endeavor—indeed, on all aspects of life.

As a consequence of the pervasive influence of religion in so many aspects of human endeavor, students of religion and society have observed that in traditional societies religion was never isolated. That is, nothing within the given society was perceived as nonreligious or profane. Every meaningful act was seen as religious or sacred. Professor Robert Bellah of the University of California at Berkeley argues that in the West the split between the sacred and the profane or the differentiation of religion from other aspects of life did not really begin until about the time of the Protestant Reformation. He refers to that period as "early modern." Beginning with the early modern period onward to the present, religion has become more and more differentiated from Western culture. Thus, for example, it is no longer assumed that an American is a Protestant, whereas it is still largely assumed that a Thai is a Buddhist.

The question has been asked, "Can someone understand a religion in which he or she does not believe?" As the previous discussion of the nature of religion indicates, belief in the truth claims of a religious tradition is not a prerequisite for engaging in its study or even for understanding (i.e., making sense of) its beliefs and historical forms. The study of religion, however, does demand empathy and sympathy. To engage in the study of another religion for the purpose of proving that one's own is superior can only result in a distorted understanding of that tradition. Or, for that matter, if one who professes no religious belief approaches the study of religion with an inhibiting scepticism, then the beauty and richness of religion will be lost. For the believer, the study of another religious tradition should enhance his or her own faith-understanding; for the nonbeliever (i.e., agnostic), the study of religion should open up new dimensions of the human spirit.

The objective study of religion should be undertaken because of its inherent significance—because the understanding of cultures and societies, indeed, of humankind, is severely limited when such study is ignored. The study of our own tradition from its own particular creedal or denominational perspective is justifiably a part of our profession of faith. However, such study should not close us off from a sympathetic understanding of other religious traditions. Rather, such inquiry should open us to what we share in common with other religious persons, as well as to what is genuinely unique about our own religious beliefs and traditions.

Is the study of religion relevant today? The authors of this series believe the answer is a resounding "Yes!" The United States—indeed, the world—is in the midst of a profound transition period. The crisis confronting nations today cannot be reduced merely to economic inflation, political instability, and social upheaval. It is also one of values and convictions. The time has passed when we can ignore our crying need to reexamine such basic questions as who we are and where we are going—as individuals, as communities, and as a nation. The interest in Islam on the part of many American blacks, experimentation with various forms of Asian religions by the "Age of Aquarius" generation, and a resurgence of Christian piety on college campuses are particular responses to the crisis of identity through which we are currently passing.

The serious study of religion in the world today is not only legitimate but necessary. Today we need all of the forces we can muster in order to restore a sense of individual worth, moral community, and value direction. The sympathetic study of religion can contribute toward these goals and can be of assistance in helping us to recover an awareness of our common humanity too long overshadowed by our preoccupation with technological and material achievement. As has been popularly said, we have conquered outer space at the expense of inner space.

But why study non-Western religions? The reason is quite simple. We no longer live in relative isolation from the cultures of Asia and Africa. As a consequence the marketplace of ideas, values, and faiths is much broader than it used to be. We are in contact with them through popular books and the news media, but for the most part our acquaintance is superficial at best. Rather than looking at the religions imbedded in these cultures as quaint or bizarre—an unproductive enterprise—we should seek genuine understanding of them in the expectation of broadening, deepening, and hopefully clarifying our own personal identity and direction. The study of religion is, then, a twofold enterprise: engaging the religion(s) as it is, and engaging ourselves in the light of that religion.

The Argus Communications Major World Religions Series attempts to present the religious traditions of Judaism, Christianity, Islam, Hinduism, Buddhism, China, and Africa in their unity and variety. On the one hand, the authors interpret the traditions about which they are writing as a faith or a world view which instills the lives of their adherents with value, meaning, and direction. On the other hand, each volume attempts to analyze a particular religion in terms of its historical and cultural settings. This latter dimension means that the authors are interested in the present form of a religious tradition as well as its past development. How can Christianity or Judaism speak to the problems confronting Americans today? What are some of the new religions of Africa, and are they displacing traditional beliefs and world views? Can Maoism be considered the new religion of China? Is traditional Hinduism able to cope with India's social, economic, and political change? The answers to such questions form a legitimate and important part of the content of the series.

The author of each volume is a serious student and teacher of the tradition about which he or she is writing. Each has spent considerable time in countries where that religious tradition is part of the culture. Furthermore, as individuals, the authors are committed to the positive value the proper study of religion can have for students in these times of rapid social, political, and economic change. We hope that the series succeeds in its attempt to present the world's religions not as something "out there," a curiosity piece of times past, but as a subject of study relevant to the needs of our times.

A Present-Day "Happening"

The parade had just ended when my wife and I, with several friends, arrived in Beigang to see the celebration of the goddess Matzu's birthday, but there was still plenty of excitement. All along the main street we could see colorful floats depicting scenes from Chinese history and literature—tableaus composed of beautiful women in colorful, traditional costumes and strong men brandishing weapons of a bygone day. There were roles too for boys and girls, whose proud parents and relatives seemed sorry that the parade had ended.

As we strolled along the side streets leading to Matzu's temple, we often had to dodge a series of palanquins, or god-carriages, carried by men who trotted boisterously through the streets as firecrackers burst around them. Each palanquin carried the image of the goddess who was being honored by this wild ride and who in turn honored each home she passed. The air was thick with firecracker smoke, so thick in fact that a man with a small bellows ran along with each palanquin, blowing the smoke away from the bearers so they could breathe a little easier.

We arrived at the temple to find hundreds of people milling about its courtyard, talking, looking for the greatest attraction, all enjoying themselves immensely. What attractions were provided? Well, some people were gathered around a woman who was in a trance and was writing in a tray of sand the messages she received from the spirit world. At another spot sat a man whose back had been pierced with long brass skewers which resembled very thin knitting needles. Various objects were tied to the skewers so that considerable weight pulled against his skin, but he too was in a state of trance and seemed to feel no pain. People were making offerings at many small shrines—lighting joss sticks (sticks of incense), bowing, and placing the sticks before images or ancestral plaques.

On one side of the central hall I found a small alcove from which I could observe the scene without being too obvious. Several attendants dressed in ordinary street clothes stood around the main altar with a Buddhist priest in yellow robes who was chanting verses from Buddhist scriptures. This was not a Buddhist temple, but he was there and chanting away, even though nobody paid much attention to him.

A group of forty to fifty people came in the main entrance of the temple some two hundred feet from the main altar. With much anticipation they handed a small bundle, wrapped with pennants and decorated with flowers, across the first altar to an attendant, who passed it to a second attendant at another altar, who passed it over smoke arising from incense sticks, and so on until the bundle reached the main altar where it was placed in front of the Matzu image. After a few minutes of bowing and chanting around the altar, the attendants handed the precious bundle back across the altars until it was received by the waiting group with a tumultuous shout of joy. Their exultation was all the more striking because they had been very quiet as they waited. Holding the bundle aloft they almost danced out of the temple as another group came in and the same ceremony was enacted.

What had happened? An old man told me part of the story, I inferred a little more, and all was confirmed by a specialist a little later. These people, and other groups like them, had brought their own Matzu image from their own village temple to be "recharged" with power from the central Matzu shrine, so that the goddess's power would be more effective in their lives during the year ahead. After having the power of a local image renewed, the people carried it through the streets in a palanquin like those we had encountered earlier in the evening.

A student from our university who lived in this town in the southern part of Taiwan invited us to his home for breakfast the next morning, obviously proud that he could honor his teachers. His parents and his grandfather were there and they served us soft rice, peanuts, dried pork, and something like a cruller (a small, unraised sweet cake). The young man treated his parents and grandfather with the greatest deference, did much of the serving himself, and occasionally translated for us since the older generation spoke a different Chinese dialect than the one we foreigners had learned.

We ate around several small tables in the living room which opened out on the street. This meant that people passing by often stopped to see the foreigners eating in the Lai home. Along the back wall of the living room, facing the street, was an altar table about three feet high, five or six feet long, and a little less than two feet deep. Candlesticks were on it, along with bowls in which offerings might be placed. On the wall were pictures of the family's ancestors and one of a Buddha.

As we left Beigang to catch a small narrow-gauge train back to the main railroad line and the trip back home, we could see that most of the townspeople were returning to their daily tasks. Some of them were still making offerings at various temples, and the ancestral shrines in people's homes were still very prominent. The festival spirit lingered on as all of us returned to our jobs and homes and daily life.

In less than twenty-four hours we had encountered some of the main features of Chinese religious life:

1. Religion in China is related intimately to Chinese culture, literature, and history.
2. The birthday of a god or goddess brings thousands of people together for high-spirited celebration.
3. "God power" can deteriorate and then be revived.
4. Certain people are gifted in a way that enables them to contact the spirit world.
5. People in a trance can be physically "hurt" but seem to feel no pain.
6. A Buddhist priest may participate in the worship of a non-Buddhist god, and a Buddha's picture or image may be associated with tablets honoring the ancestors.
7. Chinese religion never gets away from the respect for elders and the veneration of ancestors.

There are many other strands in the story of Chinese religion. We encountered several of the more important aspects by participating in this "happening" at Beigang, as people from all over Taiwan came to celebrate the birthday of Matzu, "Holy Mother up in Heaven," the deity worshipped by millions of people in Taiwan and the southeast part of China. This goddess, and others like her, will be encountered in the following story of religion in China.

RICHARD C. BUSH
Oklahoma State University
Stillwater, Oklahoma

Chapter 1

The Source of the Stream
in Ancient Times

The story of religion in China is like that of a river which has a far-distant source and is fed by many smaller streams which flow into the main stream from time to time. To find the origin or source of religion in China, one must go back to archaeological records of the earliest times and to the first literature. There scholars have discovered that many of the beliefs and practices of modern-day Chinese existed in some fashion three thousand to four thousand years ago.

ANCESTORS, HEAVEN, AND EARTH

Archaeologists have excavated the grave sites of great kings of the Shang dynasty (1765–1112 B.C.) and have discovered that the kings worshipped the spirits of their ancestors in a most elaborate manner. When a king died, he was provided with weapons, bronze vessels for sacrificial offerings, cooking and eating utensils, clothing, and various other items for his comfort. Such objects have been found in the tombs, indicating that they were buried with the king so he could use them in the afterlife. Of course a king does not cook his own food, so servants to care for him along with soldiers to fight for him and wives to provide company were also buried with him. Human sacrifices died out before the end of the Shang dynasty, but during that period they were part of some royal burials.

Although the discoveries in royal tombs have received a major amount of attention, at least a few small graves have also been

Men trot through the streets carrying a palanquin
(god-carriage) with an image of the Queen of
Heaven inside.

1

excavated. In such a simple grave only a bronze dagger-axe or a pottery vessel may be found, indicating that the common people also paid some attention to the spirits of their dead, however simple the cult of ancestor worship may have been for them. There are records that the heads of clans consulted their ancestors before taking a trip or engaging in battle or some other venture. They also reported back to the ancestors the result of their actions. Although most of the sacrifices were made to male ancestors by male members of the family, there is evidence of sacrifices to queens along with kings, and of women making offerings to female ancestors in the hope of having children.

The veneration of ancestors by royal families and common people alike reveals several reasons for ancestor worship. People wanted their ancestors to be able to live beyond the grave in a manner similar to their life-style on earth; hence the living attempted to provide whatever would be necessary. A secondary motive lurks in the background: if not provided with the food and weapons and utensils needed to survive in the life beyond, those ancestors might return as ghosts and cause trouble for the living. To this day people celebrate a Festival of the Hungry Ghosts, placing food and wine in front of their homes to satisfy those ancestral spirits or ghosts whose descendants have not cared for them and who therefore may wander back to old haunts. A third motive is to inform the ancestors of what is going on at the present time, hopefully in such a way that the ancestral spirits may be assured that all is well and therefore may rest in peace. Finally, ancestor worship expresses the hope that ancestors will bless the living with children, prosperity, and harmony, and all that is most worthwhile.

In the ancient *Book of Poetry (Shih Ching),* although compiled at a much later date, verse after verse extols the ideal monarch and by inference the ideal head of a family. Note that pious devotion to the dead has a salutary effect on the living:

> He conformed to the example of his ancestors, and their spirits had no occasion for complaint. Their spirits had no occasion for dissatisfaction. His example acted on his wife, and extended to his brethren, and was felt by all the clans and states.
>
> Full of harmony was he in his palace, full of reverence in the ancestral temple. Unseen by men, he still felt that he was under inspection. Unweariedly he maintained his virtue.
>
> Though he could not prevent some great calamities, his brightness and magnanimity were without stain. Without previous instruction he did what was right; without admonition he went on in the path of goodness. [1]

Spirits of earth and grain were also highly revered. Fertility of the soil means everything to an agricultural people, so sacrificial offerings by village elders before mounds of earth just outside the villages were very much a part of the ancient scene. The fertility of the soil, as well as human fertility, was celebrated in extravagant spring and autumn festivals, since spring and autumn are the two critical times in the annual life cycle. Community leaders staged contests for crossing rivers and climbing hills, followed by ritual dances with young men and maidens issuing challenges and invitations to each other. The couples then were paired off and betrothed. Sacrifices to earth and festivals to celebrate fertility thus developed as a major element in ancient Chinese religion along with sacrifices to ancestors.

The king's ancestor obviously ranked higher than any others and therefore was called Shang Ti, or Lord Above. (*Shang* means "upper" or "above"; *Ti,* pronounced "Dee," means "a superior person" or "lord.") From this position as chief of the ancestral spirits it was but a short step to the highest place as a supreme god or deity who was approached, not only by the royal family, but by soldiers who wanted Shang Ti on their side as they went into battle and by farmers who entreated him to give them better crops.

At some point during the transition from the Shang to the Chou (pronounced "Jo") dynasty (1111–222 B.C.), the term *T'ien,* or Heaven, gradually replaced *Shang Ti* as the name for this higher power. *T'ien* originally meant something like "abode of the great spirits," and can simply mean the sky, but it clearly refers to a supreme power or fate which has some control over human affairs. Whatever the shade of meaning, every year at the time of the spring equinox (late January or early February in China), the king stood in the presence of Heaven to report what had happened in his realm the previous year. As he presented his sacrificial offerings of grain or a bullock, he petitioned Heaven to continue good weather and crops and the well-being of his people. If things had been going badly, the king went before Heaven with great anxiety because bad crops, famine, defeat in battle, or a plague meant that something was wrong and the king himself was responsible. He would then implore Heaven to end such bad times and continue him and his dynasty in power.

Apparently not all the kings were concerned in times of great difficulty. The *Book of Poetry* includes a lament over a kingdom in which both the king and his chief minister were doing nothing to reverse the downward course. The writer sees this as Heaven's punishment:

Heaven is continually redoubling its inflictions: deaths and disorder increase and multiply. No words of satisfaction come from the people, and yet you [chief minister] do not correct or bemoan yourself.

The Grand-Master Yin . . . should be aiding the Son of Heaven [the king] so as to preserve the people from going astray. [The chief minister] does nothing himself personally and the people have no confidence in him. Making no enquiry about them and no trial of their services, he should not deal deceitfully with superior men. If he dismissed them on the requirement of justice, mean men would not be endangering the common good, and his mean relatives would not be in offices of importance. . . .

O unpitying great Heaven, there is no end to the disorder! With every month it continues to grow so that the people have no repose. I am as if intoxicated with the grief of my heart. Who holds the ordering of the kingdom? He himself attends not to the government and the result is toil and pain to the people. . . .

From great Heaven is the injustice and our king has no peace. Yet he will not rectify his heart and he resists efforts to correct him.[2]

This passage reveals the belief that the king's actions, whether good, bad, or indifferent, are in some way related to the so-called Mandate of Heaven *(T'ien Ming)*. In American political life a politician who has received a resounding majority in an election claims that he has received a mandate from the people, meaning that they have empowered and authorized him to carry out his program. A ruler in ancient China claimed to have power and sanction from Heaven itself to reign over the people. Heaven's mandate was not substantiated, of course, by any vote of the people. Good times were evidence that a ruler and his dynasty continued under the mandate and deserved the continued loyalty of his subjects. Bad times were a sign that the king had lost or was losing the Mandate of Heaven and the people therefore were justified in revolting against him. So the kings and the later emperors (after 221 B.C.) were all concerned to make the appropriate sacrifices to Heaven and thus hopefully to retain the Mandate of Heaven.

In the passage quoted above there is a hint of another factor in Heaven's mandate which looms much larger in the thought of

A shrine to the earth god.

5

Confucius and Mencius, who will be considered in the next chapter. It was believed that the ruler should be a man of moral character; the loss of the mandate, signified by disorder and disaster, suggested that there were flaws in the character of the ruler and his ministers. This ethical dimension increased in importance until Mencius proposed that a king could govern with ease and confidence if he followed moral principles and considered the needs of the people.

"Sacrifices" or "sacrificial offerings," whether made to Heaven by the emperor or to ancestors and earth by the people, refer to the presentation of grain, wine, or an animal to a god or spirits. "To sacrifice" was to hold up the object (if small enough) before the altar or place of sacrifice, place it on the altar or ground set apart for the purpose, and with appropriate words address the deity or spirit, honoring him and requesting him to ward off evil and bring certain blessings. Some such ritual action as this can be found in Chinese religion from the ancient past to the present day.

Thus religion in ancient China focused on three great sacrifices—to Heaven, to earth, and to ancestors. Sacrifices to Heaven were made by the king and his officials only, although the people were aware in some sense that the ceremonies were held. This grand and glorious ceremony was discontinued after 1911, for China had become a republic and such rites were considered inappropriate. The sacrifices to earth, primarily carried out by village elders, and those to the ancestors, which must have involved all the people, touched every level of society. These last two forms of sacrifice are still practiced in one form or another in many parts of the Chinese world today.

CONSTANT CHANGE
AND HOW TO LIVE WITH IT

An understanding of the world had emerged: there were powers from above associated with Heaven such as rain and sun, and powers of the earth below such as the fertility of the soil. It follows naturally that the forces of heaven and earth should be in a state of interaction and that all of life flows from this interaction. All people have observed this process in nature, have planted and harvested their crops accordingly, and therefore developed a rhythm of life. The ancient Chinese sensed beneath this rhythm the movement of two basic forces called *yang* and *yin*. *Yang* is above, male, light, warm, and aggressive; *yin* is below, female, dark, cold, and passive. Harmonious life is a complementary interaction of male and female, darkness and light. Rain and sun *(yang)* fall on the earth *(yin)* and crops grow. The passive yields to the aggressive but, by yielding, absorbs and overcomes. The

6

result is a philosophy of continual change which is believed to explain the rise and fall of dynasties as well as the change from day to night and back to day again. The goal of this process is a harmony of heaven and earth, of man and woman, of *yang* and *yin*. Harmony between ruler and subject, among the members of the family, and in society as a whole becomes the goal of life, both in ancient China and among many Chinese today.

Now if people feel that the basic fact about life is change, they become very curious about what specific changes may occur. What are the prospects for this year's crops, for victory against the enemy, for the marriage of the king's son? To answer such questions in ancient China, kings and common people turned to divination, practices which supposedly enable one to discern or determine the outcome of proposed actions.

The kings and high officials employed the most dramatic form of divination called oracle bones, the bone actually being the under shell of a tortoise or the shoulder bone of an ox. The bone was heated until two intersecting cracks appeared. A diviner read these cracks in order to determine whether a proposed venture should be carried out or not. Quite a few of these bones have been recovered. From the inscriptions on them we know of people's hopes and fears and of their efforts to find some sense of security amid changing fortunes.

Consulting the *I Ching* (pronounced "Yee Jing," the *Book of Changes*) has proved as popular in the United States today as it was in ancient China. This ancient process of divination was a complicated affair which called for a specialist both in performance and interpretation, but the process was shortened and simplified through the years. As shown in the diagram on page 8, eight trigrams are grouped around an ancient symbol of *yang* and *yin*. The light portions in the circle are *yang;* the dark portions are *yin*. Note that there is a little bit of *yin* in the *yang* area and vice versa, and that the line separating the two areas is curved, not straight, meaning that there is no hard-and-fast line between the two. Each of the trigrams has a name and certain images and traits. Each one corresponds to a role in the family and is also related to a part of the body and to an animal.

One trigram placed over another forms a hexagram. Eight trigrams can be combined in sixty-four ways and the result is the *I Ching:* sixty-four hexagrams accompanied by cryptic comments and interpretations. Anyone who wants to know what the *I Ching* has to say about a problem or the outcome of a proposed action may construct a hexagram and look it up in the *I Ching*.

In ancient China the order and number of broken and unbroken lines in a hexagram were determined by sorting yarrow stalks from the

milfoil plant which has finely dissected leaves and white flowers. By a rather tedious process of allowing forty-nine stalks to fall in increasingly smaller piles, the diviner determined his combination of unbroken, or *yang*, lines and broken, or *yin*, lines.

Rather than follow this tedious process a modern-day student would toss three coins to determine the structure of lines. The simplest method is to decide that if two or three coins fall heads up the student gets an unbroken line and if two or three fall tail side up he or she gets a broken line. Our student tosses for the bottom line first, then proceeds upward until each line of the hexagram has been selected.

Suppose the student gets the hexagram shown on the following page. This hexagram is called *T'ai*, or peace, and is number eleven in the *I Ching*. The opening line is a judgment: "Peace. The small departs, the great approaches. Good fortune. Success." Then there is an image: "Heaven and earth unite: the image of Peace. Thus the ruler divides and completes the course of heaven and earth; he furthers and regulates the gifts of heaven and earth, and so aids the people."[3]

To interpret the hexagram, start at the bottom line, marked *a,* and read up.

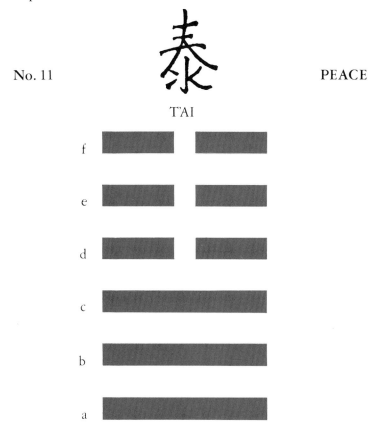

No. 11

T'AI

PEACE

a. An unbroken line at the beginning means:
   When ribbon grass is pulled up, the sod comes with it.
   Each according to his kind.
   Undertakings bring good fortune.
b. An unbroken line in the second place means:
   Bearing with the uncultured in gentleness,
   Fording the river with resolution,
   Not neglecting what is distant,
   Not regarding one's companions:
   Thus one may manage to walk in the middle.
c. An unbroken line in the third place means:
   No plain not followed by a slope.
   No going not followed by a return.
   He who remains persevering in danger

9

Is without blame.
Do not complain about this truth;
Enjoy the good fortune you still possess.

d. A broken line in the fourth place means:
He flutters down, not boasting of his wealth,
Together with his neighbor,
Guileless and sincere.

e. A broken line in the fifth place means:
The sovereign I
Gives his daughter in marriage.
This brings blessing
And supreme good fortune.

f. A broken line at the top means:
The wall falls back into the moat.
Use no army now.
Make your commands known within your own town.
Perseverance brings humiliation.[4]

The *I Ching* shows two basic patterns in the sixty-four hexagrams. If the prospects are promising as the hexagram begins, signs of foreboding appear at the end, as was the case in the preceding example. If, on the other hand, there is a gloomy picture at the beginning, then a glimmer of light can be expected at the end. Thus, no hexagram clearly says yes or no. The message is more likely to be "Go ahead, but be careful" or "Wait a while and then proceed." The responsibility, the real decision, ultimately falls back on the individual.

Scholars are not quite sure when the Chinese began to use what are called divining blocks, but the practice may well go back to ancient times. A pair of curved wooden blocks, each of which has a rough side and a smooth side, are raised in the air and dropped or thrown on the floor. Three possible combinations indicate the prospects for proposed ventures such as marriage, war, or a business deal. If one rough and one smooth side turn up, prospects for the venture are good. Two rough sides up indicate a negative answer, and two smooth sides up mean "the deity is laughing" which means one should try again. This form of divination clearly is the most popular in the Chinese world today.

Attempts to determine or "divine" the best sites for graves and buildings produced a system of geomancy, or divination based on geographic features, which the Chinese call *feng shui*, meaning literally "wind and water." A *feng shui* master had his own special techniques for surveying the contours of the land, wind patterns, and the course of water drainage. He could then advise a family as to the site which would be best protected from the elements and best adjusted to the rhythms of wind and water and other forces. For example, a house should nestle against a hillside, not sit squarely on top of it. Traditionally oriented Chinese are still inclined to consult a *feng shui* master and follow his advice if modern conditions permit.

CONCEPT OF FILIAL PIETY

While the *I Ching,* or *Book of Changes,* was being compiled during the early centuries of the Chou dynasty, other ancient classics were being written or collected. One such classic, the *Book of Poetry,* contains both popular songs and rituals used in ancient ceremonies. The *Book of Rites* gives a record of the ceremonies along with indications of how they were conducted. The *Book of History* and the *Spring and Autumn Annals,* both of which contain legendary and historical material, provide illustrations of the way kings, officials, and even some common people lived and practiced their religion. These four, together with the *Book of Changes,* constitute the Five Classics, a great treasure of information about ancient Chinese culture. Various commentaries add even more detail and interpretation, so that source material even for that ancient time is plentiful.

This literature and other sources indicate that during the early centuries of the Chou dynasty families began to place tablets or plaques honoring their ancestors in temples set apart for that purpose. Ancestral rites were held in these temples, reaching a climax at the time of the great spring and autumn festivals and on special anniversaries. A girl's father received a proposal of marriage for her in the ancestral temple. Important affairs of state were discussed and settled in the ruler's ancestral temple.

The head of the family always led the ancestral ceremonies. There were officials, even servants, who specialized in the precise form of the ritual, but they functioned as advisers to the head of the family. There was also a personator, a member of the family who supposedly was possessed by the spirit of the ancestor being honored. This personator ate and drank, asserted in behalf of the ancestor that the offerings were acceptable, and pronounced a blessing on the company assembled.

During the Chou dynasty the practice of sacrificial offerings to the ancestors was considered part of a much broader system of filial piety, which may be defined as the devotion and obedience which younger members of the family give to their elders, in particular the devotion a son gives to his father. As the *Classic of Filial Piety (Hsiao Ching)* expressed it a few centuries later, "The services of love and reverence to parents when alive, and those of grief and sorrow to them when dead—these completely discharge the fundamental duty of living men."[5] Duties to living and dead parents and grandparents blended easily, for the distinction between living and dead was not sharply defined. "The son who does not reverently discharge his duty to his father" was more detestable than the chief criminal in the state; likewise the younger brother who does not respect his elder brother.

Senior members of the family were supposed to deserve the respect rendered them and to reciprocate in appropriate ways, but their authority was supreme. Blood revenge was expected if a member of the family was killed, and one who killed in taking revenge usually was pardoned by the law. A son whose father committed a crime was expected to support and defend his father. Authority of the elders extended to the arrangement of marriages, because marriage was for the purpose of extending and continuing the family line. Romantic love found occasional, poignant expression in the *Book of Poetry* but was seldom fulfilled. Women were subservient to men. One of the first duties of a bride was to sacrifice to the ancestors of her husband's family, which meant that she owed her primary loyalty to his family as personified in her mother-in-law.

Thus the obedience to the senior members of one's family, especially to one's father while alive, and meticulous offerings to the spirits of these family members after their death became the two essential aspects of filial piety. Through offerings to ancestors there was contact with the world beyond; through loving obedience to senior family members there was involvement with the world at hand. Sacrifices to earth could be accommodated, since fertility of the soil and of the human family insured the continuity of life. Sacrifices to Heaven gave a more cosmic framework than offerings to Shang Ti, the king's ancestor who became the Lord Above.

Filial piety is therefore the primary element or main stream in Chinese religion, both in the ancient past and in the present. An amazing variety of currents move in and out of the main stream of filial piety with their varying emphases in thought and activity. Dominant among these are Confucianism, Taoism, Buddhism, and folk religion. But the main stream of filial piety flows through them all.

Chapter 2

The Confucian Current

China's greatest philosophers spoke during times of chaos and despair. The Chou dynasty flourished during its first four or five centuries, but by the sixth century B.C. serious decay had begun. The period from 480 to 222 B.C., though technically the last period of the Chou dynasty, is officially called the Period of Warring States. During this time of confusion and strife a series of philosophers struggled with basic issues in the meaning of life, and in the process they set forth ideas which were to have a profound effect on religion in China.

The philosophers in question never thought of themselves as religious leaders or founders of religious movements. Very few Chinese, scholars or common people, from that day to this have called them religious. Each of these philosophers, however, dealt seriously with the Chinese religious tradition as he understood it. The manner in which each of them interpreted or responded to the tradition had some effect on religion in China. Therefore these philosophers are interesting to anyone who studies religion in China.

THE GREAT SAGE

Confucius, founder of the school of philosophy which bears his name, died just as the Warring States period began. His name was K'ung Ch'iu and he is called K'ung Tzu or Master K'ung by the Chinese. When the first Europeans heard an honorific form, K'ung Fu Tzu, they Latinized the sounds as Confucius and that name still remains.

Confucius' long life (551–479 B.C.) was devoted to education, to teaching the students who gathered about him certain basic ethical principles which bring about a good society and responsible government. The child of a poor but respected family in the ancient state of Lu (in what is now Shantung province), he tried to make it possible for worthy young men to develop character through study. He was appointed to fairly important posts in the government of Lu in his fifties, but apparently was not allowed to put his principles into practice. Confucius, therefore, left government service and spent the

13

rest of his days going from place to place teaching the band of disciples who gathered around him. A record of some of the things he said, as these disciples remembered them, is contained in a small book called the *Analects* (*Lun Yu* in Chinese).

Confucius did not see himself as a savior or messiah with a new idea for people to follow. In his words: "I transmit but do not create. I believe in and love the ancients. I venture to compare myself to our old P'eng."[1] (P'eng was an ancient official who liked to tell old stories.) Confucius regarded himself as a transmitter, one who saw the past with its traditions as a model for the present. He was a conservative in the best sense of the word, one who sought to conserve what was best about the past, not just because it was old, but because he passionately believed that it would work in the present. It was especially important for good government and a harmonious social order to follow the way which had worked so well in the past.

What was this ancient way, or _tao_ (pronounced "dow")? First of all it was a way of proper ceremony in particular and of propriety in general. The Chinese word for this twofold way is *li* (pronounced "lee"), meaning both ritual and ceremony on the one hand, and propriety—doing things in the proper way—on the other. Following this way is what we would expect of a transmitter, a conserver of ancient values, and Confucius does not disappoint us. He loved to see a beautiful ceremony and, even more, to participate in one, wear the proper regalia, sing the right music, and, most important, do all these things with sincerity.

The most important ceremony to carry out in the proper way, according to Confucius, was the veneration of ancestors, an inescapable aspect of filial piety. He defined filial piety in words that parallel the *Classic of Filial Piety (Hsiao Ching)* and leave no doubt as to his position: "When parents are alive, serve them according to the rules of propriety. When they die, bury them according to the rules of propriety and sacrifice to them according to the rules of propriety." (*Analects* 2:5)

As to attitudes toward living parents, if a son feels that his parents are following a wrong course of action, he should remonstrate with them; but if they pay no attention to him, the son "should resume an attitude of reverence and not abandon his effort to serve them." A son should not go far from his parents, especially without telling them where he is going. As his parents advance in age a son rejoices in their long life but is concerned because another year has passed. (*Analects* 4:18–21) In these and many other passages Confucius affirmed that filial piety was a major value in his philosophy of life.

14

Confucius also stressed righteousness (*I*, pronounced "yee"). The ruler and his ministers, as well as the common people, should follow a high moral standard:

> The superior man regards righteousness as the substance of everything. He practices it according to the principles of propriety. He brings it forth in modesty. And he carries it to its conclusion with faithfulness. He is indeed a superior man! (*Analects* 15:17)

Confucius had in mind one who brings himself under control, who blames himself rather than others, who goes beyond the outward show of righteousness.

The heart of Confucius' system of values lies in his unique combination of loyalty and reciprocity which results in humanness or a sense of humanity. Loyalty, first of all, includes loyalty to one's family, to the ruler, and to the way of life previously described. The Chinese character *chung* (pronounced "joong") is made up of two characters, one meaning "middle" or "center" (中) and the other meaning "heart" or "mind" (心), thus (忠). Therefore loyalty means the centering of the heart on a basic purpose or person.

Reciprocity, the second factor, has to do with giving and receiving, so the Chinese *shu* (pronounced like the English word "shoe") corresponds to the concept of altruism. The character has three parts: *nu* (女) meaning "woman," *k'ou* (口) meaning "mouth" or "an opening," and *hsin* (心) meaning "heart." Woman, who receives the seed and gives forth the child, is the symbol of warmth and love. Through the mouth or any opening things come in and go out. And the heart likewise symbolizes a human being's capacity to give and receive, and thus to be "all heart." All of these ideas are caught up in the Chinese word *shu*, which carries the meaning of reciprocity quite simply and profoundly in the character itself (恕).

Now these two values, loyalty and reciprocity, come together according to Confucius in one supreme value with the meaning of humanity, humanness, or being human or humane. The Chinese word is usually written *jen* in English, but the pronunciation is much closer to "ren." The simple pictograph for man (人), also pronounced "ren") is turned on its side and the character for two (二) is added, thus producing the character and concept of humanity,(仁), or what should prevail when two humans get together. To set one's mind on humanity is to be free from evil. It is the summit of virtue in the Confucian value system.

Confucius also talked about such virtues as sincerity, seriousness, wisdom, and faithfulness. The way of life he advocated should include all of these. One who follows such a way, who upholds the values just described, is a princely man, a superior man, who influences all around him. The princely man is not necessarily a man of royal birth. He is a man of virtue.

At this point, however, someone is certain to raise the question: What does all this have to do with religion? Beyond these beautiful moral maxims is there anything specifically religious? First of all, it has been noted that Confucius did say that ancient rituals for ancestors and other spirits should be followed, although it is said that he "never discussed strange phenomena . . . or spiritual beings." (*Analects* 7:20) He once said that wisdom was to "devote yourself earnestly to the duties due to men, and respect spiritual beings, but keep them at a distance." (6:20) Indeed, one of his disciples, Chi-lu, asked him about serving spiritual beings and about death. Confucius replied, "If we are not yet able to serve man, how can we serve spiritual beings? . . . If we do not yet know about life, how can we know about death?" (11:11)

When Confucius was ill, a disciple reminded him of the advice to pray to spiritual beings. He replied, "My prayer has been for a long time." (7:34) On the one hand he said that the four seasons run their course without Heaven saying anything (17:19), but on the other hand he claimed that Heaven had produced the virtue that was in him (7:22). When his disciple Yen Yuan died, Confucius exclaimed: "Alas, Heaven is destroying me! Heaven is destroying me!" (11:8) He also spoke of the superior man as one who stands in awe of the Mandate of Heaven (16:8), that life and death, wealth and honor, follow upon the same mandate (12:5), and claimed that he himself at the age of fifty knew the Mandate of Heaven (2:4).

Several of the passages quoted in the preceding paragraphs have been interpreted by some to mean that Confucius was religious and by others to mean that he was not. Most Chinese have interpreted them in the latter way, so that "keeping the spirits at a distance" means that he did not believe in spirits, and that Heaven means nature and not a god. On the other hand, to "keep the spirits at a distance" may mean a healthy respect for powers that human beings do not fully understand. There can be little doubt that Confucius saw Heaven as a vital power affecting human life, whether he believed in Heaven as a personal god or not. To concentrate on human, social problems, to give priority to service to one's fellow human beings, hardly means that one does not believe in spirits. It suggests rather that one regards the human situation as the most pressing problem for a person with an ultimate concern for human values.

When the passages quoted above are considered along with the many other sayings of Confucius, he may be seen as a man who, rooted in tradition as he surely was, assumed the presence of ancestral spirits, the spirits of earth and grain, and the more impersonal but nonetheless powerful Heaven. Although he spent very little time talking about these powers and never developed any systematic doctrinal statement about them, he assumed their existence and believed that they affected human existence in profound ways. Therefore men were obligated to deal with heaven, earth, and ancestors in the proper manner with traditional rites and ceremonies. The performance of sacrificial rites must be accompanied by moral values, however, so Confucius shifted his attention and the attention of his disciples to the world of human relationships, to the problems of the family and society and government. In such a way he made the contribution for which Chinese people and many others around the world remember him. So it has been with many leaders past and present who are called religious: accepting the existence of realities or powers beyond the human, these people have received inspiration and support to live the common life and interpret its meaning in ways that are not forgotten.

IDEALIST AFFIRMATION BY MENCIUS

Confucius' most outstanding follower—Mencius, or Meng Tzu (371–289? B.C.)—born just over a hundred years after the death of Confucius, adhered essentially to the teachings of the Sage but at certain points developed those teachings with great insight. Mencius affirmed the same values Confucius did but highlighted the following four: humanity, righteousness, propriety, and wisdom. Confucius had talked about wisdom but had not emphasized it as much as some of the other values he advocated.

Mencius pushed beyond Confucius when he asserted that these four values or virtues result from natural feelings which all human beings have from birth. According to Mencius, all people have a feeling of sympathy for others, especially those who are in pain or trouble, and from this feeling arises humanness or humanity. All people feel ashamed when they have done wrong or dislike what is wrong; from this feeling of shame and dislike arises righteousness or the determination to do the right thing. All people have a feeling of

17

respect and reverence for that which is superior; from such a feeling arises the virtue of propriety, of engaging in the proper ritual. All have a feeling of right and wrong, and from this feeling wisdom develops.

One is tempted to argue with Mencius on several points. For example, there are people who do not seem to be troubled at all by the suffering of others, and many people do things which would have made their forefathers feel very ashamed if they had done them. So at least this question may be raised with Mencius: How can you say that these feelings are inborn in all men and women?

Mencius probably would reply that those who do not feel sympathy or shame have not developed their innate feelings. He would then put forth his basic conviction that people are alike in the "natural capacity endowed by Heaven. The abandonment [of the capacity for good] is due to the fact that the mind is allowed to fall into evil."[2] Mencius' classic example is that of seeing a child about to fall into a well. Would not anyone rush to grab the child?

Thus in Mencius there is a developed doctrine that is only implicit in Confucius, namely that people are by nature originally and essentially good. In dealing with others, therefore, people should try to appeal to that basic goodness. The king should remember that the common people have feelings similar to his; if he treats them well, they will be loyal to him and serve him. All human relationships are concerned with trying to develop and bring to maturity the goodness that is already in people. It is neither a case of restraining those who are basically evil nor a matter of getting sinners to repent.

Although Mencius' idealism may be regarded as terribly naive, one cannot help but admire his unshakable faith in humanity. He takes an extremely idealistic stand for righteousness, one of the four major virtues in his classification. What about taking a big government job which will bring several luxuries but will also involve breaking the moral code? What if the king should be so angered by a refusal of the office that he might put the refuser to death? Mencius says:

> I like fish and I also like bear's paw. If I cannot have both of them, I shall give up the fish and choose the bear's paw. I like life and I also like righteousness. If I cannot have both of them, I shall give up life and choose righteousness. I love life, but there is something I love more than life, and therefore I will not do anything improper to have it. I also hate death, but there is something I hate more than death, and therefore there are occasions when I will not avoid danger. . . . Therefore there is something men love more than life and there is something men hate more than death. It is not only the worthy ones alone who

have this moral sense. All men have it, but only the worthy ones have been able to preserve it.[3]

Mencius' uncompromising stand for righteousness and the other values of the Confucian way of life earned for the collection of his sayings a place in the literature called the Four Books. Two other works from the last centuries of the Chou dynasty which discuss the moral life for individual, government, and society—the *Doctrine of the Mean* and the *Great Learning*—are also honored. Written by unknown but devoted followers of Confucius, these two works along with the *Analects* and the *Book of Mencius* comprise the Four Books, which stand beside the Five Classics as the authoritative word of life for Confucian Chinese.

VARIATIONS FROM THE CONFUCIAN PATTERN

Two men in ancient China would have agreed on many points with Confucius and Mencius, but they differed on enough critical issues to put them on the fringe of the Confucian tradition. The first of these was Mo Tzu (pronounced "Mwo Dz") who was active from about 479 to 438 B.C., thus right after Confucius and almost a century before Mencius. The phrase for which Mo Tzu is remembered reads: "Universal love and mutual benefit." As he explains it, universal love means that one should regard other people's countries, families, even other people themselves just as one regards his own country, family, and self. Then people would love each other, work together, be peaceful and harmonious. The benefits would be obvious: "The strong will not overcome the weak, the many will not oppress the few, the rich will not insult the poor, the honored will not despise the humble, and the cunning will not deceive the ignorant."[4]

Why should anyone quarrel with such a philosophy? One might say it is too "iffy"—*if* people would love, work hard, drive safely, and so on, then the world would be a lot better. The Confucians, however, objected on other grounds. Universal love would undercut filial love— the love of a son for his father, the love of the younger for the older in the family—and it would destroy the particular loyalty that subjects feel for their ruler.

The Confucians objected even more to the way Mo Tzu pointed to "mutual benefit" as an incentive for doing good, for loving others. The Confucians argued that one should love, or practice humanity, or do the right thing because it is good or right, not because of what one gets out of it. These Confucians probably were a little hard on Mo Tzu, who was trying to point out good reasons to be gained from following the way of

universal love, but they were trying to be rigorously honest. The moral life should be followed for its own sake, they said, and many of them throughout Chinese history refused to sacrifice principle for benefit, as seen in the last quotation from Mencius.

Mo Tzu wrote convincingly against war, as might be expected. He also attacked the standard practice of mourning for three years after the death of a loved one, saying it was too expensive and that it interfered with ongoing life and work. Quite a few followers came along to advance his teachings, but the movement died out after about three hundred years, leaving his book to be criticized by Confucians and, many centuries later, to be admired by Christian missionaries who saw a parallel between the teachings of Mo Tzu and Jesus.

The second notable thinker on the fringe of the Confucian tradition was Hsun Tzu (pronounced "Syun Dz"), who lived about 298–238 B.C., or just after Mencius. Flatly disagreeing with Mencius, Hsun Tzu maintained that human beings are by nature evil. With much to tempt them and few resources to sustain them, people naturally reach out for personal gain. Therefore they have to be restrained and controlled by education, laws, and police; otherwise chaos will result. Of course, Mencius and the orthodox Confucians also believed in education, but for them education was a means to develop people's natural goodness. For Hsun Tzu, education was needed to restrain the naturally evil impulses of human beings, and that is quite different. Chinese kings and officials usually have claimed that they have followed or wanted to follow Mencius' view that human nature is good, but they have had laws, a police force, and horrible jails for those whose lives might support Hsun Tzu's position.

Hsun Tzu seems not to have believed in any kind of supreme divine power, yet he advocated the worship of gods and spirits through rites and ceremonies. He thought participation in religious rituals "*as if* the

Simplicity and serenity are the hallmarks of this Confucian temple.

spirits were present" had subjective value because it made everyone feel good and thus helped to overcome evil impulses. It made no difference whether there really were any spirits or not, and he apparently did not think any such powers existed.

The important thing was for people to do something about the dangers they faced. If a storm is coming, he advised, take precautions for your house and family and see to it that the animals are sheltered. There is no point, he said, in making offerings to the spirits to keep the storm from coming.

Hsun Tzu and his followers, called Realists, have provided the rationale for a school of legalists who set to work devising laws to keep people in line. Although Confucian scholars have followed Mencius' teaching on human nature, they have tended to follow Hsun Tzu's interpretation of Confucius' sayings on religion. Thus, Chinese today say that Confucius did not really believe in spirits but thought they should be worshipped as if present.

In spite of variations and conflicts in philosophy, made all the more confusing by the chaos of warring states, Confucianism finally triumphed as the standard school of thought in China. Early in the Han dynasty (206 B.C.–A.D. 220) an ardent Confucian scholar named Tung Chung-shu was appointed chief minister and used his position to make Confucian teachings the standard for government. Officials should be learned men, and their education should come from the study of books, which, naturally, should be the Five Classics and the Four Books. As a result practically every government official from 136 B.C. to A.D. 1911 had to master this literature. The examinations for this civil service system tested one's knowledge of this ceremonial, moral, and philosophical literature which emphasized rites to heaven, earth, and ancestors. To be an official was to be grounded in the classics and in the ideal philosophy of government taught by Confucius, Mencius, and the scholar class.

For better or for worse, the Confucian philosophy which was adopted as the philosophy of the state followed the ideas of Hsun Tzu, that spirits probably did not exist but the worship of them made for harmony and order. This became the purpose for continuing sacrifices to heaven and earth, a state cult centering in the belief that China was the embodiment of all under heaven that was noble and good. Since Confucius was made the patron of the scholar class, he received continuing honor from the scholars and from other people. In a sense they were honoring a great man, but in another sense they were venerating one who was more than a man. It is possible, therefore, to speak of a "cult of Confucius," although it is doubtful that the man himself was actually worshipped. Regardless of whether he functioned as a god or not, his ideas permeated government and society to the extent that traditional China is Confucian China.

To summarize, the Sage Confucius and his followers definitely affirmed filial piety and the veneration of ancestors, and therefore the importance of the family. Over and beyond ancestral rites, Confucians are known for their love of all ceremony, assuming of course that it is done seriously and with sincerity.

The moral life is also a major concern for Confucians. The virtues to be followed are spelled out carefully and profusely illustrated with stories and examples. The social order and good government both depend heavily on moral conduct by everyone from the king down to the common citizen. Remember that this is based on a belief in the natural goodness of human nature; therefore your moral conduct toward me will evoke as a matter of course my moral conduct toward you in return.

The rituals to be followed and the living of a moral life are part of the harmony of heaven and earth and even help to further and complete that harmony. Those who see Confucianism as "morality *only*" miss this point. It is not just a case of living a good life according to moral rules. People who live a moral life participate in the universal harmony of heaven and earth and thus are related to powers beyond them and within them which give ultimate meaning to human life.

The rituals and the moral code to be followed are based on tradition. Although Confucians were not "hidebound," they had little use for innovation. They had an almost blind faith that those who followed the traditions of the past would be able to cope with the problems of the present. Western attitudes, like the attitudes of many contemporary Chinese, are different from those of traditional Chinese, but one must not forget that for well over two thousand years their insistence on ancient moral principles and ceremony gave Confucian leaders and many Chinese people the strength to stand firm in chaotic times. As the *Doctrine of the Mean* expresses the thought of Confucius:

> The Emperor Wu and his brother, Duke Chou, were eminently pious men. Now, true filial piety consists in successfully carrying out the unfinished work of our forefathers and transmitting their achievements to posterity.
>
> . . . [Preparations for the rites are described.]
>
> To gather in the same places where our fathers before us have gathered; to perform the same ceremonies which they before us have performed; to play the same music which they before us have played; to pay respect to those whom they honored; to love those

who were dear to them—in fact, to serve those now dead as if they were living, and now departed as if they were still with us: this is the highest achievement of true filial piety.

The performance of sacrifices to Heaven and Earth is meant for the service of God [Shang Ti, the Lord Above]. The performance of ceremonies in the ancestral temple is meant for the worship of ancestors. If one only understood the meaning of the sacrifices to Heaven and Earth, and the significance of the services in ancestral worship in summer and autumn, it would be as easy to govern a nation as to point a finger at the palm.[5]

Junior high school students perform a predawn dance in celebration of the birthday of Confucius.

Chapter 3

The Taoist Current

In contrast to the proper, ceremonial, moral Confucians, the Taoists with their relaxed "Who cares?" manner seem like a weird counter-culture. It may be that the Taoist current in the Chinese religious stream contradicts not only the Confucian way but practically everything associated with religion.

As we approach Taoism (*Tao* is pronounced "Dow"), we must be prepared for the strange and mysterious, even for a bit of humor. In the first place no one really knows when and how Taoism began. It was once thought that Lao Tzu, the Old Master, was a minor official who gave his philosophy to a gatekeeper before "going West," and thus founded Taoism, but most scholars think the story is legendary. There are traces of a few people before the time of Confucius who were unconventional, who followed little more than the *yin-yang* philosophy of change and doubted everything else. They might be called the first Taoists, but the evidence is not all that clear.

Second, it is not known who wrote the first Taoist book, the *Tao Te Ching* (pronounced "Dow Deh Jing"), formerly attributed to the above-mentioned Lao Tzu and written between the sixth and fourth centuries B.C. The title of this very short book can be translated "The Book of the Way and Its Virtue" or "The Book of the Way and Its Power," so one may expect to find in it a way of life and a method for following that way.

In the third place, however, readers are immediately dumbfounded by the first line of this classic: "The Tao which can be named is not the Tao." To name or describe Tao is to miss it, so how can it be discussed? Before we get completely enveloped in mystery we can note that the character for *Tao* (道) refers to a road or a path, so we are speaking literally of a roadway which can or should be followed.

THE WAY OF FLOWING WITH NATURE

As we try to find something in the *Tao Te Ching* to grab hold of, we discover several intriguing similes which hint at the meaning of Tao:

an infant, the female, a valley, an uncarved block, and water. Confucians uphold the educated, mature gentleman; Taoists prefer the spontaneous infant who cries when hungry or wet, smiles when fed and dry and loved. Confucians clearly are male oriented; the *Tao Te Ching* turns to the female who receives, who "by going underneath conquers the male." Many religious people speak of a mountaintop experience as the greatest; Taoists seek for the valley, the ravine of the world which receives all things. Most people prefer finely carved and polished figures; the uncarved block suggests original simplicity instead. And finally Tao resembles water, not necessarily because of its cleanliness and purity, but because water seeks the lowest place.

On a more abstract level, emptiness is upheld as an important quality: only because it is empty can a bowl be used. The *Tao Te Ching* also talks of all life as a mixture of being and nonbeing and of nonbeing as the original quality of life. Darkness and obscurity characterize Tao, thus adding to the sense of mystery.

We still cannot say precisely what Tao is or means, but we do have these hints: it is a way associated with simplicity, with the natural and spontaneous side of life, with that which is low and receives. Recalling the *yang-yin* concept of interacting male and female, aggressive and passive, upper and lower forces of life, a concept which Taoism emphasizes, we might compare Confucianism to the *yang* and Taoism to the *yin*. The similes of the *Tao Te Ching* certainly indicate such a *yin* view of life or feeling about life.

Now that we have this somewhat vague notion of what Tao might mean, we are faced with the question of how one follows Tao. The literal answer again surprises us, for we read in the *Tao Te Ching* of no action or nonaction, the literal translation of the Chinese phrase *wu-wei*. When we get down to cases, however, we find that it does not mean just sitting around doing nothing. "Nonstriving" is closer to the real meaning, the kind of action that is spontaneous, without effort or strain. The picture of a natural-born athlete comes to mind, swinging a bat or swimming effortlessly. I remember a friend telling of the joy of using hammer and saw and other simple tools as he made repairs on his house. "The point," he said, "is to let the tools do the work; don't struggle with them as you pound and push and pull." I think the *Tao Te Ching* is speaking of a life-style in which an individual works and plays and lives according to his or her own nature rather than trying to follow some artificial model which a Confucian or anybody else might propose.

Both the *Tao Te Ching* and later Taoists proposed nonstriving as the way for officials to rule a people. There are lines in the book which even suggest keeping people in ignorance so they will not know there is anything better to strive for, which is Taoism at its worst. Those lines, however, are stated deliberately in an extreme manner to shock the Confucian bureaucrats. Thomas Jefferson's idea that a government is best which governs least, pushed to its extreme, is closer to the real meaning. Tao is the way of nature and all people may allow that way to pervade their lives and thus realize a better life for themselves as individuals and as a community. Perhaps the most poignant expression of early Taoist teaching comes from this little book's assertion that the conquering general at a victory celebration should behave as if he were at a funeral.

Although such a person as Lao Tzu may never have lived, scholars are fairly sure that a man named Chuang Chou (pronounced "Jwang Jo") lived in China during the fourth century B.C., that he served as a minor official but declined promotion to a higher post, and that he wrote the book which bears his name, *Chuang Tzu,* or Master Chuang. He was a man obviously sensitive to the mystery of life, but, far from trembling at the mystery, he could accept it and smile.

Chuang Tzu was impressed with the sounds of the world such as the wind and the human voice. He was fascinated by dreams, as the following story indicates.

> Once I, Chuang Chou, dreamed that I was a butterfly and was happy as a butterfly. . . . Suddenly I awoke, and there I was, visibly Chou. I do not know whether it was Chou dreaming that he was a butterfly or the butterfly dreaming it was Chou. Between Chou and the butterfly there must be some distinction. This is called the transformation of things.[1]

In the face of mystery can one say "This is this" or "That is that"? No, says Chuang Tzu, there remains only the transformation of things, the endless process of change. Remember *yin-yang* interaction?

If Tao means change, if change is the way of life, then ways are found to adjust to that process. If people are uprooted, they come to see the advantages in such a move and accept it. Death, the ultimate uprooting, is not to be feared; it follows life as surely as life follows death. Chuang Tzu tells the winsome story of a man about to die: the wife and children are weeping and wailing, but a friend, through whom Chuang Tzu speaks, exclaims, "Don't disturb the transformation that is about to take place!" He apparently demonstrated in his own life this attitude toward death, for after Chuang Tzu's wife died a friend came to call. There was Chuang Tzu sitting on the ground, singing as he beat out the rhythm on an earthen bowl. You can just hear the friend saying, "After all your wife has done for you, how can you behave like that?" Chuang Tzu replied:

> When she died, how could I help being affected? But as I think the matter over, I realize that originally she had no life; and not only no life, she had no form; not only no form, she had no material force. In the limbo of existence and non-existence, there was transformation and the material force was evolved. The material force was transformed to be form, form was transformed to become life, and now birth has transformed to become death. This is like the rotation of the four seasons, spring, summer, fall, and winter. Now she lies asleep in the great house [the universe]. For me to go about weeping and wailing would be to show my ignorance of destiny. Therefore I desist.[2]

A further understanding of the life process is reflected in this personal testimony about death. An energizing, "material force," which has evolved from a mixture of being and nonbeing, takes on form, then life, then death, and then the cycle repeats.

The Taoist way is to adjust to or fit into this process of change, to see that there is no "this" or "that," only the unity of all things. "The Universe and I exist together." One becomes aware of the Tao in all things and thus lets things take their course. There is no need to strive for fame, or plan and execute strategies, or manipulate people to get things done. Rather true Taoists "travel where there is no sign," exercise what they have received from nature, live out the Tao which is within all people and within all things.

These two books, *Tao Te Ching* and *Chuang Tzu,* give an indication of Taoist origins and philosophical foundations. Although other books presenting a somewhat different view of life appeared in following centuries, it is important to ask what the ideas found in these particular books have to do with religion.

Both books are based on what has been called a mystical philosophy or wisdom. Philosophy is used here in its literal sense—the love of wisdom, which leads to the development of wisdom in the inner man. It is not philosophy in the sense of logical theory, rational ideas, or statement and proof of hypotheses.

Mysticism usually refers to the knowledge of, communion with, or perhaps even union with the divine. A Christian mystic, for example, is one who claims to have a vision of God or Christ leading on to an experience of oneness with God or of intimate communion with Christ. The early Taoist books say practically nothing about a god figure, and the few references to a "Creator" should not be interpreted as meaning a personal, creator god.

The legendary Lao Tzu and the barely historical Chuang Tzu seem to have had deep, spiritual insight into the hidden nature of life resulting in a "vision" of Tao as the way of nature and of life. People may adjust to, relate to, or be permeated by this Tao so that they actually feel that they are one with Tao. This may be regarded as a mystical experience for it touches the depths of religious experience, especially when defined as people's approach and/or response to the powerful reality (in this case Tao) which they experience as having a profound effect on their existence. Confucianism is a more formal approach to realities such as heaven or spirits. Early Taoism was more of a yielding response—a fitting into, and opening up to, the ongoing, continually changing life process.

POPULAR OR RELIGIOUS TAOISM
ENTERS THE STREAM

Shortly after the time of Chuang Tzu, Taoist people became fascinated with the possibility of prolonging life, both as the continuation of one's earthly life for several hundred years and as immortality following death. The Chinese had long believed that there was a lighter soul or spirit that continued after death, so Taoists tried to encourage or develop this lighter aspect of their lives by both breathing exercises and lighter diets. Certain types of air, such as the morning mist in springtime or the *yin* clouds in autumn, were to be inhaled and then circulated through the body by vigorous exercises. Lighter foods were believed to accomplish the same goal, so Taoists avoided heavy cereals, meats, and the like, and tried instead to live on the lightest vegetables and flowers, or on tiny portions of gold, mercury, and jade.

The mention of such substances as gold and mercury leads to the practice for which these Taoists were most famous—namely, alchemy, the melting of metals in order to discover the elixir or substance of immortality. Gold and cinnabar (mercuric sulphide) were the more promising candidates since they were supposed to last forever, so the Taoist masters proceeded to melt down either of these substances and came up with a "pill of immortality." A symbol of this pill can be seen in Taoist temples today. Looking at the symbol is considerably safer than taking it, for several Taoist masters and at least one emperor died from taking cinnabar.

Other bizarre practices developed. One of the earlier ones called for jumping into a fire so as to ascend to heaven like a flame, a practice soon discarded for obvious reasons. Other Taoists thought that by engaging in sexual intercourse but withholding semen they could retain the life fluid and thus live forever.

These are only a few examples of methods Taoists used to prolong life. Although their actual success was limited, there is a real galaxy of "immortals" who are honored and even worshipped in folk Taoism. Whether these immortals lived a long life or not is not important. They are believed to have possessed remarkable powers which have lifted them above ordinary mortals, so they are worshipped as "immortals" and function as deities.

In addition to these immortals a series of deities appeared during the last two centuries B.C. (the Former Han dynasty). Tao itself was personified and deified with the amazing designation "Celestial Venerable of Mysterious Origin." Much later he became known as the "Pure August One" or Yu Huang, the Jade Emperor, the name by which he is known today. Two other deities called "August Ruler of the Tao" and "August Old Ruler" were added to make a Taoist trinity. The last one is depicted as a white-haired old man who was regarded as an incarnation of Lao Tzu. Variations in this trinity occur, but the Jade Emperor is constant.

Thus people have deities to whom they can pray as well as practices by which they can actively seek the Tao and its power. This power can actually be appropriated for one's use, whether to gain immortality or drive demons from one's home or from a human being. This may seem strikingly different from the earlier mystical philosophy, but it may also be seen as a more activist operation in the total Taoist framework.

Religious professionals were needed to carry out these activities, so a Taoist specialist, called a *Tao Shih* today, appeared on the scene. In ancient China there were male and female shamans who, it was thought, could handle the spirit power and could transmit messages from the spirits to ordinary human beings. The *Tao Shih* (pronounced "Dowshr," and meaning literally "Tao professional") usually was a specialist in alchemy, knew the rituals for exorcising demons from buildings and people, and of course knew the rituals for the great festivals such as those described later in this chapter. The community obviously regarded him as a charismatic individual, one who was "gifted" by a higher transcendent power.

Taoist literature of the first few centuries A.D. is full of stories of outstanding personalities. Ko Hung (pronounced "Geh Hoong") was an alchemist who lived for eighty years (254–334) and wrote a classic of popular Taoism entitled *Pao-pu-tzu*, "The Master who maintains the simplicity of his nature." Although trained in the best Confucian tradition, he gave most of his life to experiments with cinnabar in

32

order to find the right drug to give immortality. The drug by itself, however, was insufficient, he claimed; it must be accompanied by good works. This moral stress was ignored by some of his fellow Taoist masters.

During the Later Han dynasty (25 B.C.–A.D. 220) the first Taoist groups were being organized. Increasing chaos at the end of the Han dynasty was the setting for a man named Chang Chiu who had received a revelation while still a young man that the age of Universal Peace *(T'ai P'ing)* would appear in A.D. 184 after ten years of political and natural catastrophes. The *yin-yang* idea can be seen here in the alternation of periods of calamity with periods of peace.

Chang Chiu preached to the people who gathered around him that the misfortunes of the time were due to human sin, so all his followers were to make public and private confession of their sins and drink sanctified water. If they did so, they would be immune to danger from gods, spirits, or men. Should any of them die in battle, it was assumed that they lacked faith or had not confessed all their sins. People gave up their belongings which were then distributed to the poor. Chang's followers built roads and bridges by voluntary labor and quickly built up a mass movement in east central China that was intended to be peaceful. The government regarded the demonstrations as a rebellion and attacked. Chang Chiu died in 184, the year when Universal Peace was to have dawned, but it took another twenty years for the government to wipe the movement out.

Chang Tao-ling, of the late second and early third centuries A.D, claimed to have concluded a universal treaty with all demons and spirits and thus to have gained control of their powers. He himself could produce charms which would protect people and exorcise the demons. He passed these powers on to his son Chang Heng and then to his grandson Chang Lu. This is said to be the origin of the Taoist papacy, a line of succession in Taoist leadership which continues to the present.

An organization which Chang Tao-ling established has a unique name derived from the generosity his followers were supposed to express. They were to give to the head priests five *tou* (pecks) of rice, so the group came to be known as *Wu-tou-mi Tao,* "Five Pecks of Rice Tao."

Numerous Taoist sects have appeared through the centuries. Members are admitted in a secret ceremony in which they are said to pledge their lives in loyalty. The disciplines practiced are also kept secret but definitely have included combat skills. Since many of the sects attracted men opposed to the government, they were a constant threat. Both national and provincial officials were highly suspicious and constantly on guard against a rebellion. There were revolts, but for the most part the groups were peaceful in orientation and devoted to the continuation of the secret rituals that meant much to them. Five of these sects survive in Taiwan today.

ACTS OF CELEBRATION

As various Taoist groups arose they collected rituals for various occasions. The Tao Tsang, a collection of Taoist sacred literature describing these rituals, is a kind of growing Bible which has been collected over the centuries. Practically no one knows this material in its entirety, but Taoist priests have become specialists in certain portions of it. The rituals described in the Tao Tsang are performed down to the present time. Especially when these rituals are enacted as part of a community festival called a *chiao,* people experience a real sense of celebration. Some of the festivals are held only once in sixty years and so are extremely special.

Preparation for a festival begins years in advance as community leaders are organized, the temple repaired and refurbished, and special symbols collected. People engage in acts of purification and penitence for a month before the festival begins; the more devout abstain from meat and increase their acts of charity to the poor. Other acts of merit such as performing deeds of filial piety, reciprocating good deeds, and repaying debts are common in the weeks before the festival. Wool, leather, and white objects associated with death are avoided, and guards are set up around the temple to keep anyone wearing such items from entering.

A host of gods and goddesses are invited to be present at the ceremonies. These include Buddhas and Bodhisattvas from Buddhism and deities from the folk religious tradition, as well as Taoist deities like the Jade Emperor and deified founders of Taoist sects. Shrines are set up for these visiting deities by wealthy families, and the smaller images from village shrines and temples are placed on a platform before the main temple. Human visitors including foreigners are invited, as are ancestors and souls from the underworld, all of whom may be liberated from bondage by participation in the festival.

Taoist professionals who know and can recite the sacred texts must be enlisted to lead in the ceremonies. A high priest and several subordinate priests are brought to the local temple. The whole group of priests, in addition to musicians to accompany the rituals, receive fees for their services. All are beautifully robed in elaborate vestments with red as the primary color. The chief priest who stands in the central courtyard of the temple has a cantor on his right who represents *yang* forces and an assistant cantor on his left who represents *yin* forces. As the two cantors alternate in singing the liturgy, they symbolize the alternating and interacting forces of *yang* and *yin*.

The rituals last for three, five, seven, or nine days, depending on how well the townspeople have funded the festival. The following is a summary of an extended account of a three-day festival,[3] which is about all that people can afford these days.

The first day's activities begin with a welcome to the gods and spirits with considerable attention devoted to exorcism of evil spirits from the temple and grounds. Rituals of merit and repentance express the theme for the day. At day's end, around midnight, a ritual to renew the community is performed as symbols of five life-giving elements are planted in the five directions of the temple.

The second day includes a welcome to the gods and spirits, and more scriptures of merit and repentance are read. A prominent element on the second day is a series of "audiences" with Taoist deities. The climax comes in the evening when paper lanterns constructed and set up by families before the festival are taken to the river bank or seashore. The lanterns are attached to small rafts, set afire, and then released to move out to sea or down the river to the sea. The blazing lights from the lanterns are an invitation to the ancestors to come for the feast on the last day.

The third day also begins with a welcome to the gods and spirits, but there is a special rite to invite and pay homage to the Jade Emperor. The Tao Ch'ang ritual itself then completes the rituals of renewal and brings the Three Pure Ones, or Taoist trinity, into a compact with the villagers. A memorial containing the names of all villagers and their petitions, with an account of the festival, is presented to a host of Heavenly Worthies inside the temple and then to the Jade Emperor outside. Souls from the underworld are given a great banquet, followed by a rite which releases all souls from hell. The gods are thanked and sent back to their sacred homes. There is a carnival with side shows, and a local opera and puppet shows are staged. Each family is given a yellow document to place over the family altar as a notice to gods and men that the ritual for renewal of the whole village, including that particular family, has taken place.

As the blazing lanterns drifted into the sea, so the Taoist current merged with the continuing stream of Chinese religion. The Taoist current itself has at least two strands: the quiet, mystical philosophy which suggests so gently that one should blend with the process of transformation; and the active handling of the power of life so as to prolong it. Beyond the differences in Taoism itself, both basic Taoist types seem contrary to restrained, orderly Confucianism with its moral and ceremonial concerns.

The distinctions made here are important, but they are not rigid. Men who have been Confucians most of their lives, stalwart citizens and family men, tend to slip back to nature and "sit loose" in their declining years. The *yang* side of their nature gives way to *yin* as they turn essentially into Taoists. Confucian ceremonial is reserved and modulated; Taoist ritual is offbeat and sometimes shocking. Each honors the ongoing harmony of heaven and earth.

Confucians think highly of nature in spite of a certain artificiality. Taoists object to moral rules, but their way of following the Tao produces a moral person. The Tao of Chinese religion is a pathway which both the Confucian and the Taoist can follow.

(top) A Taoist temple, miles from any city or town.
(bottom) A series of altars, characteristic of the interior of Taoist temples.

Chapter 4
The Character of Buddhism in China

The third major current in Chinese religion began in the small kingdom of Magadha in northeast India in the sixth century B.C. How Buddhism, a very Indian religious movement, came to China and became a part of it, and what happened to Buddhism and religion in China as a result, is one of the great miracle stories in the history of religions.

Gautama the Buddha, also known as Prince Siddhartha and as Sakyamuni (called "Shr-jya-muni" in Chinese), who lived from 563 to 483 B.C., was uncomfortable in the kingly family to which he was born. Leaving his wife and child, he set forth to seek the meaning of life as a wanderer in the forest. Various teachers and holy men failed to answer his questions. Finally in meditation under the Bo tree he realized that all life is suffering and that suffering is caused by our craving and attachment to things and even the people we love. If that is the case, then those who cut off the craving and attachment are released from suffering and discover an indescribable calm and peace called Nirvana. The way to achieve this goal is long and rigorous, but human beings can follow this way themselves without help from gods or Buddhas. Groups of monks and nuns arose to spread the teaching of the Buddha and to provide an example for lay followers.

BUDDHISM BECOMES A PART OF CHINA

You may read in greater detail about the Buddha's way and its growth and development in another volume in this series. In this chapter we shall leap over early developments in India and begin our story by pointing out that by the time Buddhism spread to China amazing variations in doctrine and practice had occurred. Actually a distinct branch called Mahayana, or Great Vehicle, had developed which was ultimately to take root as the prevailing form of Buddhism in China. Mahayana Buddhism has many Buddhas in addition to the

one so central to earlier Indian Buddhism. There are also Bodhisattvas, enlightened beings who have earned entrance into Nirvana but choose to postpone that step in order to make their own merit available to suffering creatures. Help from both Buddhas and Bodhisattvas is available to all people high and low, so the older, "do-it-yourself" approach is transcended by a sense of grace, of dependence on "other power." For example, in the Pure Land school of Mahayana Buddhism, attention focuses on the Buddha Amitabha ("A-mi-t'o-fo" in Chinese), Lord of the Western Paradise or Pure Land, who has vowed to save all who call upon him in true faith and devotion. Those who say "Praise to Buddha Amitabha" with such devotion go immediately to the Pure Land at death, so a colorful and beautiful heaven in effect replaces Nirvana as the goal. Many Mahayana groups proclaim that all beings will be saved, in fact that all beings will become Buddhas, so there is a doctrine of unlimited, universal salvation.

The Buddhism which first found its way to China had many other features, some of which evoked real hostility from the Chinese. The monks shaved their heads and that seemed to the Chinese to be doing injury to the body one had received from parents. Monks and nuns were criticized as lazy because they lived a remote life in their monasteries and nunneries and so were not available for military service or for work on farms or in the home. The worship of relics seemed abhorrent to Chinese, especially to the Confucians. The fact that monks would not bow down to king or emperor was a terrible offense. Doctrines such as the emptiness of all things appeared abstract to the point of meaninglessness.

The worst thing of all about Buddhism to the Chinese was the celibacy and therefore the childlessness of the Buddhist monk. Since he had no sons, there was no one to keep the ancestral fires lighted. Consider the plight of a Chinese man whose son became a monk. What would happen to the father after he died? The son probably would continue the ancestral rites for his father and grandfather as long as he, the son, lived, but when he died the line was broken. There would be no descendents to keep the ancestral fires lighted for the family, and they

An ancestral shrine in a Buddhist temple, Taiwan.

would become hungry ghosts with no one to quiet and satisfy their restless journeying to find food and rest.

Various documents indicate that opposition to Buddhism sometimes was mocking and sarcastic, at other times bitter and intense. Chinese Buddhists, however, did not give up. They found they could use Taoist terms to make their Buddhist doctrine of emptiness more palatable. (Remember the empty bowl and the complementary notions of being and nonbeing in the *Tao Te Ching?*) Buddhists claimed that a young man who became a monk built up a great store of merit on which his father and grandfather might draw in the afterlife. Precisely at this point early Buddhist teachers in China scored their greatest gains. Although Chinese believed in and worshiped their ancestors, they had only a vague idea of what happened to these spirits in the afterlife. The Buddhist doctrine of *karma* filled in the gap, for *karma* means "deed" or "act" and involves the further belief that a person's actions in this life determine what will happen to that person or someone else in a future existence. Buddhists therefore argued that a person's ancestors were inheriting the results of their past deeds. One must, by his own deeds while alive, try to build up good *karma* for his own hereafter and in the process aid his ancestors in their struggle after death as well. Doing Buddhist good deeds, of course, would aid immeasurably both now and later on.

The skill with which Buddhists answered the criticism of their religion by the Chinese is matched by the heroism and courage of both Indian and Chinese monks who brought Buddhism from India to China. Men who exemplified the Bodhisattva spirit of self-sacrifice and compassion carried the message of the Buddha and the scriptures north from India through Central Asia and then along the Gobi Desert to China. Chinese monks inspired by this message went to India to study further at places where the new teaching began. They obtained further scriptures, made pilgrimages to sacred shrines, and studied under famous Indian monks.

A few bits of evidence indicate that Buddhism had appeared in China by the first century A.D., but the movement of Indian and Chinese monks just described really proceeded from the second century onward. By that time routes for the silk trade had opened up which could be followed, but it was still a long and dangerous journey. Sufficient water and food constituted a real problem in arid lands; bandits would rob or kill even a monk. Mountains and deserts were a challenge to the hardiest traveler, and monks are not noted for physical strength. There is no reason to doubt the wry joke that later travelers on this route, both monks and traders, found their way by the skeletons of those who had preceded them. (See map on page 45).

The growth of Buddhism in China was aided by Confucianism's decline from the second century on. It was a period of great activity in Taoism, but Buddhism was able to relate to Taoism, both in the idea of emptiness already noted and in practices such as meditation. It was relatively easy to place Buddhist images alongside Taoist images of the Jade Emperor and Lao Tzu. The Buddhist message of relief from suffering, as expressed in compassionate Buddhas and Bodhisattvas, appealed profoundly to people who had suffered greatly as the Han dynasty collapsed at the beginning of the third century A.D.

The order of monks, the *sangha*, was thoroughly organized in China by the end of the third century. Among the famous monks of this early period was Tao An, who specialized in the study of wisdom literature, worked on the rules for the religious life, and built a great monastery. His disciple, Hui Yuan, founded the White Lotus Society which is the beginning in China of the Pure Land school. Then the illustrious Kumarajiva, from Central Asia, was captured by a Chinese army and taken to the Chinese capital about A.D. 400. He was held captive for eighteen years, but Chinese scholars helped him translate the scriptures in his cell.

Minor persecutions in the fifth and sixth centuries, attempting to force monks and nuns to return to lay life, did not last long. Such oppression probably occurred because Buddhism was becoming strong enough to be noticed, but in the long run it did little to halt the advancing Buddhist movement. Buddhism had become a real part of Chinese culture and was on the eve of its greatest flowering in the seventh and eighth centuries.

The T'ang dynasty (A.D. 618–907) ranks as one of the major cultural epochs in any civilization, particularly in the areas of art and architecture, literature, and religion. Representatives of many faiths gathered at the capital of Changan, often at the invitation of the emperor, including groups of Nestorian Christians and followers of the cult of Mithra which stems from the Zoroastrianism of ancient Persia. Confucian scholars were there, of course, along with Taoist priests, but for the first two centuries and more of the T'ang dynasty, Buddhism with its beautiful temples, outstanding monks, and devoted lay followers played the major role.

The monks were well trained in the literature of Buddhism. In order to be ordained they had to demonstrate their ability to comment or lecture on at least some of the texts and were expected to be proficient in meditation. Many of them went about as storytellers and debaters, telling stories from the Buddhist scriptures to the masses and engaging in debates with each other on the fine points of Buddhist doctrine.

Some of them had to take charge of the temples and proved themselves to be able administrators and businessmen. Since monks and nuns were often given land of their own, were provided with robes by wealthy laymen, and were fed and sheltered, a monk's role in T'ang dynasty China was a far cry from what it had been five centuries earlier.

It was the monks' participation in the ongoing life of Chinese communities, however, that won a place in Chinese society for the monks and in Chinese culture for Buddhism as a movement. The stories they told often evoked fear of hell, delight in the Buddha's teaching, and wonder at the marvelous events which occurred in the life of the Buddha and his disciples. One of the most popular stories told by the monks was of Moggallana, an Indian *arhat,* or saint, who won enlightenment by his own disciplined effort. In the story Moggallana attains such power that he rescues his mother from hell. She then wanders about as a hungry ghost for a time, becomes a dog, and then is reborn in heaven. Villagers hearing this story were filled with admiration for the monk and were enthralled by the power of the *arhat.* Fearful that they too might find themselves in hell, they were thrilled by the mother's release and hoped that the same would happen to them. How wonderful to have a monk around who can tell a story like that!

The chief function fulfilled by Buddhist monks in Chinese society, almost from the beginning to the present time, has been their ministry when death occurs. Not only have they recited the scriptures at funeral ceremonies, but at intervals following the funeral Buddhist monks are called in to say masses for the dead. Remember that one's existence after death, according to Buddhist teaching, is determined by the deeds that one has done in this life. In popular belief the afterlife is something like an obstacle course through hell as one goes from this judge to that, from a fiend who saws you in half to another who roasts you over a spit. Those who can afford it call upon the Buddhist monk who helps the ancestors over such hurdles. The gifts given to the monks and to monasteries for such services help also to build up merit for those who have gone on and to enhance the image of the living as examples of filial piety.

The monasteries often became wealthy as a result of income from the land and from services rendered, but many monasteries used the income to help individuals and communities by such deeds of charity and compassion as caring for the aged and the sick, the poor and the hungry. Hospitals and dispensaries were set up to care for the sick. What we call "soup kitchens" for the hungry and homes for the aged were established. There were places for weary travelers to take a bath

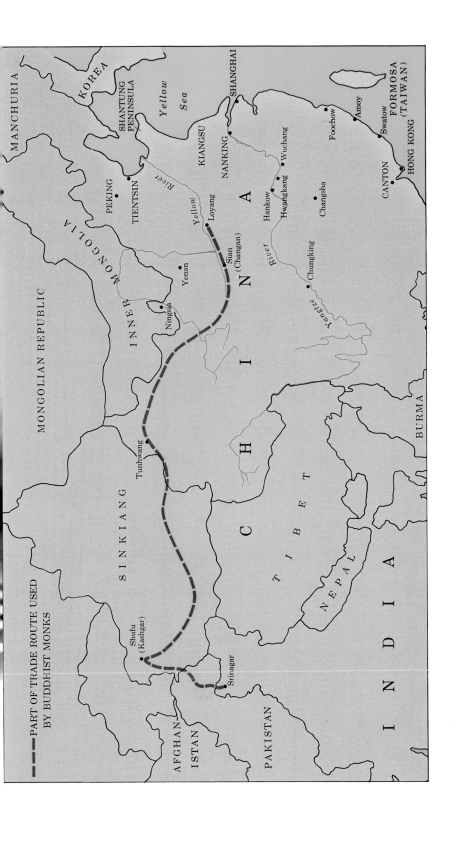

PART OF TRADE ROUTE USED
BY BUDDHIST MONKS

MANCHURIA

KOREA

SHANTUNG
PENINSULA

Yellow
Sea

SHANGHAI

FORMOSA
(TAIWAN)

Amoy

Foochow

KIANGSU

NANKING

Swatow

HONG KONG

CANTON

Wuchang

Hwangkang

Hankow

Changsha

Chungking

MONGOLIA

INNER

PEKING

TIENTSIN

River

Yellow

Loyang

Sian
(Changan)

C H I N A

Yenan

Ningsia

River

Yangtze

MONGOLIAN REPUBLIC

SINKIANG

Tunhwang

T I B E T

BURMA

Shufu
(Kashgar)

Srinagar

NEPAL

AFGHAN-
ISTAN

PAKISTAN

I N D I A

and rest a while. Monastic funds were used not only within the monastic precincts, but were often used to help communities build roads and bridges, dig wells, and plant trees. The institution was so comprehensive that Kenneth Ch'en, on whose work much of this discussion is based, writes that the Buddhist temple and the monastery of which it was a part formed for the faithful

> an institution which touched on almost all aspects of his life. It sustained him with spiritual comfort, assisted him with economic aid when needed, offered him entertainment on various occasions to lighten his daily toil, provided him with opportunities for social companionship, and took care of him when he was ill, aged, or infirm.[1]

The glories of Buddhism during China's T'ang dynasty are reflected in the Buddhist inspired art and architecture of the period. Sculpture, painting, and architecture in particular express in the most refined and delicate manner the spirit of a faith which had become thoroughly Chinese. Great sums of money were spent on both images and temples, but their great simplicity remains.

Such preeminence could not last forever. In 845 the Emperor Wu Tsung, who had turned to Taoism, decreed a full-scale persecution or suppression of Buddhism which included destruction of temples, melting down of statues, and the return of thousands of monks and nuns to lay life. A Japanese visitor to China, Ennin, reported that in 845–846, the year of his visit,

> more than 4,600 monasteries are being destroyed throughout the empire; more than 260,500 monks and nuns are being returned to lay life and being subjected to the double tax; more than 40,000 temples and shrines are being destroyed; several tens of millions of ch'ing of fertile lands and fine fields [belonging to monasteries] are being confiscated. . . .[2]

Ennin noted that Nestorian Christians and Zoroastrians also received harsh treatment.

The motives for the persecution of Buddhism are fairly clear: the government wanted the lands and wealth of the monasteries, and it wanted taxes and labor from about one-third of a million people who had been exempt from one or both. Furthermore, Taoist and Confucian leaders had attacked Buddhism as a foreign religion responsible for the corruption of the empire. Practices such as reverence for relics of the Buddha were scorned as superstitious. These motives, along with political considerations, led to the persecution. Buddhism never quite regained the great splendor it had achieved during those golden days, but the patterns of life described above were deeply established and were revived under a succeeding emperor. Many of the schools or denominations discussed below are also part of a continuing Buddhist stream.

BUDDHIST TRENDS OF LIFE AND THOUGHT

By the time of the T'ang dynasty several schools or denominations had developed in Chinese Buddhism. Although representatives of one school might differ from or debate with representatives of another, there were few instances of antagonism or of one school saying "Ours is the only way." Therefore it is hardly appropriate or accurate to speak of these groups as sects. They are regarded as schools of thought and life and practice, willing to live and let live.

Some of these schools were transferred from India, some arose from Chinese soil; but each of them either gave special attention to a particular Buddhist text, like the *Lotus Sutra,* or emphasized a doctrine such as the void or a practice like meditation. There were schools, specializing in a study of monastic discipline, which have died out. An esoteric school in which a secret wisdom was communicated through mystic symbols died out during a persecution in the ninth century, but it still survives in Japan as Shingon, the "True Word."

Although these and other schools have disappeared, there are others which have had a profound influence on Chinese Buddhism and a few which continue to play a major role in Chinese Buddhist life. There are two thought or idea schools—the Consciousness Only school and the school of the Void. The first maintains that the moments of experience have no real existence but are known in a Consciousness Container. The second maintains that all is emptiness, that nothing has any permanent existence, but this void or emptiness is seen as an openness in life in which one is free from absolutes. If you are puzzled by these strange ideas, you can perhaps see why most Chinese Buddhists have been puzzled and have left such schools of thought to a very few intellectuals.

Two other schools are noteworthy for their universalistic teaching that all beings will be saved, in fact, that all beings will become Buddhas. One is T'ien T'ai, named for the mountain on which it originated, which regards the *Lotus Sutra* as its scripture. In this text a host of Buddhas and Bodhisattvas proclaim the message that they will not rest until all creatures have been saved. The other is Hua Yen, meaning Flower Garland, the name of the sutra which is read and studied. In addition to the teaching of universal salvation there is the message of the unity of all things. All *dharmas,* meaning in this context all moments or phases of existence, can be found in a speck of dust.

Since, according to this concept of unity, that which is truly real is believed to have no substance, then all things can come together as one.

All these schools fade into insignificance, however, when considered alongside the two which do survive in strength at the present: the Meditation school, called Ch'an in China and Zen in Japan, and the Pure Land school. The former appeals more to the upper classes and to intellectuals, the latter to the common people.

Ch'an tradition begins with the story of Bodhidharma, who had been the twenty-eighth Ch'an patriarch in India and came to China where he became the First Patriarch. In an interview Bodhidharma told the emperor that there was no merit in the emperor's good deeds, that Buddhist doctrine was empty, not sacred, and that he (Bodhidharma) didn't even know his own name. Probably no one objected to ending that rather unproductive conversation, and Bodhidharma retired to a monastery where he meditated for nine years with his face to the wall. The legend that his legs dropped off just might be true!

A shrine dedicated to Kuan Yin, the Bodhisattva who hears the cries of the world.

49

Four more patriarchs followed before Hui-neng (637–713, or early in the T'ang dynasty) became the Sixth Patriarch. A contest was held by the Fifth Patriarch to see who would succeed him to office. One monk submitted a poem which read as follows:

> The body is the tree of perfect wisdom.
> The mind is the stand of a bright mirror.
> At all times diligently wipe it.
> Do not allow it to become dusty.

Hui-neng's poem read a bit differently:

> Fundamentally perfect wisdom has no tree,
> Nor has the bright mirror any stand.
> Buddha-nature is forever clear and pure.
> Where is there any dust?[3]

The insight expressed in this poem won Hui-neng the office of Sixth Patriarch of the Ch'an school in China.

It should be clear by this point that Ch'an is not just an ordinary kind of religion. This is confirmed by a classic statement attributed to Bodhidharma:

> A special transmission outside the scriptures;
> No dependence upon words and letters;
> Direct pointing to the soul of man,
> Seeing into the nature and attainment of Buddhahood.[4]

Bodhidharma told the emperor that good deeds were not important. Both Hui-neng and the third line of the last quotation suggest a focus on something within man which, according to the last line above, opens up the Buddha nature. And that is just about what Ch'an Buddhists claim, namely, that the Buddha nature is within a person and that it can be realized through meditation. The Buddha nature cannot be learned from books, even from the Buddhist scriptures, for that would be a useless dependence on words and letters. It must be transmitted from person to person.

The transmission process itself is also unusual. If a Ch'an master thinks that his disciple is depending too much on logic or reason, the master may hit the disciple on the head in order to "knock out" the attempt to think rationally and thus open the way to an awareness of one's true nature, the Buddha nature within. The disciple may ask a question like "Who is the Buddha?" and the master replies, "I know how to play the drum, rub-a-dub, rub-a-dub." That seems to be a way of saying that the meaning of Ch'an cannot be attained through question and answer; the reply is an inane non sequitur to force the disciple to give up his logic and reason and break through to his true nature.

Just what Ch'an is cannot be explained, for the Ch'an masters insist that one must personally experience the gloriously liberating realization of the Buddha nature. What has been said here comes from the Ch'an masters themselves as they try to say what Ch'an is *not*. One can see how this Buddhist school has an appeal for those people in China, Japan, or any part of the world who are no longer satisfied with scriptures, rituals, and creedal formulations. Ch'an is not for every person, but, for those who are inclined toward meditation and are willing to risk the unusual, Ch'an has made and is making its appeal.

The school which makes by far the greatest appeal to vast numbers of ordinary people, however, is the Pure Land school. Its teaching and practice, as pointed out at the beginning of this chapter, is simple and easy to grasp. Buddha Amitabha, the Lord of the Western Paradise, has vowed to save every creature who calls on him with sincere faith and devotion. One who says "Nan wu A-Mi-T'o-Fo" (Praise to Buddha Amitabha) reverently and sincerely, really believing it, will be reborn in the Pure Land at death. The scriptures describe this Western Paradise with glowing superlatives as a place of great beauty with trees and streams and as a place of lovely sounds with bells ringing and birds singing.

In view of this simple faith and act of worship it is not surprising to find Pure Land temples in constant use and frequented by large numbers of people. The refrain "Nan wu A-Mi-T'o-Fo" may be heard at almost any time, chanted in a high and slightly nasal tone to the accompaniment of bells and rhythmic drumming on a hollow wooden fish. If an actual service is being conducted, priests and/or nuns move about in crisscrossing lines as they chant lines from a sutra. Candles, and in these days electric lights, illuminate the images; colorful banners and offerings of flowers and fruit grace the altars. The result is an indescribable mixture of brooding seriousness and effervescent gaiety. No wonder so many people are attracted to it.

One should not suppose that people join one of these schools or denominations as Americans join a church. A particular temple may be a Pure Land or Ch'an temple, and people may choose to be associated with one or the other, but there is little competitiveness or rivalry. The old saying—"T'ien T'ai and Hua Yen for doctrine, Ch'an and Pure Land for practice"—suggests the gentle way in which Chinese can bring these different schools into complementary relationship.

Most of the activities of Chinese Buddhists these days are not limited to any school but can certainly be found in the Pure Land context. The closest rival to the Buddha Amitabha is the Bodhisattva Kuan Yin whose image can be found almost anywhere—in temples dedicated to her or to a Buddha, in a simple roadside shrine, or at a home altar. There are many Bodhisattvas ("P'u Sa" in Chinese), beings who have postponed Nirvana in order to help suffering creatures, but Kuan Yin outshines them all.

The full Chinese name of this most popular Bodhisattva is Kuan Shih Yin P'u Sa (first two syllables pronounced "Gwan Shr"), which means literally "Hearing World's Cries Bodhisattva." Kuan Yin therefore is the Bodhisattva who hears or regards the cries of the world. She is depicted as a gracious Chinese lady and is approached especially by women who desire children or for aid in childbirth. Women also approach Kuan Yin in behalf of their husbands who are away from home and in danger or in behalf of their children facing examinations at school. Above all Kuan Yin is the symbol of compassion, sacrifice, and love; offerings and prayers to her lift up this motif to a central place in Chinese Buddhism.

This note of compassion may be seen also in Buddhist attitudes toward animals, fish, and all living creatures. Buddhism shares with Hinduism and Jainism a belief in *ahimsa,* noninjury to all living beings, with the consequence that devout Buddhists do not eat meat. There are certain restaurants, often operated by Buddhists, which specialize in vegetarian dishes; and many monasteries provide vegetarian meals to pilgrims and visitors. A Chinese friend of mine saw abstinence from meat as the mark of a true Buddhist. Many years ago he was denied a visa to come to the United States for graduate study because a few people in his native country told American Embassy officials that he was a Communist. I tried to intercede for him but without success. Wistfully he exclaimed to me, "How could I be a Communist? I haven't eaten meat for fifteen years!" His logic may be hard to understand but not his conviction: although he had been reared in a Buddhist family and had frequented the temple from early childhood, he dated his being a Buddhist from the date he stopped eating meat.

Another expression of compassion for all creatures was expressed when the Hong Kong Buddhist Association went around to fish shops and restaurants where fish were kept alive in small tanks of water until just before they were to be killed and cooked. Buddhist representatives bought enough fish to be noticed, kept them in water until they could hire several boats, and then took the fish out in the harbor and released them. The Buddhists presumably took these actions because (1) they had genuine feelings of compassion and (2) they believed that they gained merit for themselves in the life beyond the grave.

Buddhists carry out many other activities to do good and gain merit. They support literature societies which publish Buddhist literature.

They make gifts to temples, monasteries and monks, Buddhist schools, and various programs of relief work, exemplifying again the note of compassion. Each year in May the Buddha's birthday is celebrated with very colorful services, processions, and public meetings, all of which call for contributions by the laity. People believe they gain merit as they support such causes, service is rendered the community in many instances, and such activity serves to bind the Buddhist faithful together.

Another important figure in Chinese Buddhism typifies the Chinese adaptation of Buddhism. Buddha images from India or Southeast Asia depict a Buddha who is thin, serious, even austere. Some of this austere iconography is carried over into Chinese Buddhism, but there is one Buddha in China who is completely contrary to this image and that is the Buddha-to-come, or "Mi Le Fo." He sits in a slumped position so that his big belly protrudes in a most obvious manner. A wisp of a smile can be seen on his lips, suggesting that all the food he has eaten has delighted his gourmet mentality as well as his stomach. The detached reserve of other Buddhas has shifted to a focus on this world, a world that the Buddha-to-come enjoys immensely. The pragmatic, this-worldly orientation of the Chinese has absorbed the austere, serene stance of early Buddhism, while at the same time providing ways to gain merit in order to get through that other world. The reference to a miracle story at the beginning of this chapter was not as farfetched as it sounded. A "foreign religion" has become an integral part of the Chinese scene.

Chapter 5
Popular Folk Religion

Chinese folk religion brings together practically all aspects of religion considered thus far in this book. Ancient sacrifices to heaven, earth, and ancestors, Confucian affirmation of moral and ritual values in that tradition, Taoist "reversal" to spontaneous oneness with nature or attempts to gain long life, Buddhist introduction of ways to salvation by following several paths—all these currents flow into the main stream which can be designated folk religion.

Folk religion or "popular" religion, wherever it is found, refers to a "people's" religion, a combination of beliefs and practices which people follow and have in some sense developed themselves. It is not so much individuals but communities, societies, clans, and families who, over long periods of time by a very gradual process of selection, have built up a pattern of belief and practice which seems to them to meet their needs. This pattern may reflect the orthodox or standard teaching and way of life of a particular religious group such as Buddhism or Taoism, but more often than not it represents a people's adaptation of official teaching and practice. To those who live outside the pattern which prevails in a given community or region, the folk religious configuration may appear contradictory or just plain weird, but to people within the circle everything hangs together because the resulting whole meets their needs. If some belief or practice loses value or ceases to be useful, they can substitute a different belief or practice into the total pattern without any great difficulty.

It has already been noted how Confucianism and Taoism, although different in many fundamental respects, can be seen as two sides of the same coin and can alternate in the lives of people or in the developing culture of China. It has also been noted that Buddhism used Taoist imagery and terminology as it fitted into the Chinese scene. Although Chinese in general and Confucians in particular thought Buddhism undercut family ties and destroyed filial piety, Buddhists were able to incorporate certain patterns of filial piety into Buddhist life and thought and become a more acceptable part of the ongoing Chinese religious stream. Therefore, even if one thinks of Confucianism,

Taoism, and Buddhism as the "three religions of China," which I think is inadequate, there is a mixing and blending of the three which can be called folk religion. Chinese folk religion is much more than this, and some of that "more" will be explored in the remainder of this chapter.

THE GODS OF FOLK RELIGION

Folk religion adds to the Chinese religious stream many new deities which people worship in order to gain the benefit of divine power. In this case the divine power is believed to have been expressed in certain heroes of the past who have done marvelous deeds. When crises struck people in later times, they turned to those ancient heroes, made offerings, or prayed for relief from plague or disaster, often as a last resort. If favorable results occurred, they proceeded to make gods out of the heroes and erect temples to them. The effectiveness of the hero-turned-god in meeting human need is the criterion for continued devotion, as the following examples will show.

Perhaps the most prominent of such deities is a red-faced deity called Kuan Kung (pronounced "Gwan Goong"). Back in the early third century a patriotic military hero called Kuan Yu and two sworn companions fought bravely in behalf of the fading Han dynasty. They failed, but their great courage was remembered by the people and extolled in a novel, *The Romance of the Three Kingdoms*. In several crisis situations through the centuries people prayed and made offerings to this ancient hero, and the crises were either averted or came to an early end. For example, in 1813 rebel troops broke into the Forbidden City in Peking but fell into complete disarray and were captured when they saw an image of Kuan Kung. Countless temples were erected in his honor. Kuan Kung, as he is called in his deified form, is invoked for victory in battle, faithfulness in business contracts, financial success in business dealings, and even as a god of literature. He has become a model of patriotic, civic, and family virtue, so that his magical powers are enhanced by the highest moral qualities. He presides over a large, new temple erected during the late sixties at a busy corner in Taipei, Taiwan, and seems to have hundreds of worshippers any day of the week.

A similar example is that of a general of the fourteenth century who has been deified as the Fierce General Liu because he seems to be able to drive off swarms of locusts with his sword. Many temples are built to him in the eastern part of China. One of these, near Shanghai, was destroyed in the nineteenth century by a semi-Christian rebel group which was opposed to idolatry. About ten years later great swarms of locusts attacked the county and proved uncontrollable by ordinary measures. The county magistrate fasted and prayed to General Liu. Flocks of crows appeared and drove the locusts into the sea. The incident was regarded as a miracle and the temple was speedily rebuilt.

The most prominent example of a deified hero in the contemporary scene is that of a deified heroine by the name of Matzu. It was her birthday celebration story that began this book. She is the prominent deity all along the western shore of Taiwan where she is worshipped by fishermen and their families. The story as told by the Taiwanese people goes that Matzu was a young girl whose family home was on the seashore in Fukien province where her ancestors had lived. Several boats of fishermen were at sea when a tremendous storm struck and they could not find their way home. Sensing this, Matzu set fire to her house and the fishermen were guided home by the light of her blazing home.

There are other stories of Matzu saving fishermen by appearing to them out of the clouds, extending her hand to them and offering help. Another story tells how she saved people during a time of plague by going to the mountains to gather herbs which saved many lives. In similar ways she protected the Chinese ambassadors on a mission to Korea, resulting in an imperial decree that a plaque be hung in her honor at the Matzu temple at Meichow, her birthplace. Several such miracles are attributed to her in her lifetime. Although her parents tried to arrange a marriage for her when she came of age, she refused, saying that she had dedicated her life to helping the poor and suffering. The story goes that she died in the year 988 at the age of twenty-eight and ascended directly into heaven, but returns to aid any of her devotees who need her.

Some of the complexity and scope of folk religion can be seen in a survey which C. K. Yang made of temples in five provinces in different parts of China about 1949.[1] Only in two communities did he find a sizable number of Buddhist and Taoist temples. In six other communities he found Buddhist and Taoist temples greatly outnumbered by temples to other gods. Just to give an idea of the bewildering array, the following paragraphs list deities according to their function and give names only when they are well known.

1. First of all there are the deities related in some way to family life: those approached by women in the hope of having children, such as Nai-nai and Niang-niang and the Bodhisattva Kuan Yin; those who uphold kinship values such as the "spirits of chaste women and filial children," "spirits of filial sons and dutiful brothers," and "spirits of martyrs for chastity"; and gods who bring happy marriages such as the cowboy and the weaving girl, worshipped in star constellations.

2. Next come the gods for community prosperity and protection: those approached to overcome fire and flood, the sea, and locusts; those associated with roads, bridges, and ferry docks; distinguished officials such as Kuan Yu (Kuan Kung) and friends; various gods of wealth, justice, or literature. Preeminent in this regard is Ch'eng Huang, the city god, who presides over the total welfare.

3. Then there are the deities of heaven and hell: those associated with heaven such as the Taoist Jade Emperor, heavenly Buddhas, various elements such as sun and rain, and the sky gods; those who dwell in the underworld, which includes the earth god; those who judge the souls of the dead such as the city god, homeless spirits of the dead, and a Buddha who saves from hell.

4. There are deities who aid agriculture: the old gods and spirits of earth and grain, headed by T'u Ti Kung; gods of the elements mentioned above, plus a god of sweet dew and a god of drought; the gods of rivers, floods and sluice gates, trees, horses, and fire; and over them all is Shen-nung, who in Chinese mythology is the creator of agriculture.

5. Other trade deities are represented, most of them functioning in a way similar to the patron saints of medieval trade guilds in Western Europe: Lu-pan, the famous god for trades of carpentry and construction; T'ien Hou, the queen of heaven for sailors and fishermen; and to bless all the trades, Ts'ai Shen, the god of wealth.

6. The gods of healing and health have many temples dedicated to them: there are gods who specialize in healing certain parts of the body like the eyes or in healing certain diseases like smallpox and the epidemics resulting from them; there is Hua-t'o, the patron of doctors and health, and Yao-wang, the god of herb medicine; finally Yo-shih-fo is the Buddha of healing.

7. Impossible to categorize are a wide variety of deities and spirits which can only be listed: deities who drive away demons, goddesses of mercy such as Kuan Yin, several Taoist fairies, "a general on a white horse," "a spirit incarnate in a fox," the five apparitions, the nine saints. There are temples dedicated to no particular deity but known simply as old temple or new temple; one is called "the temple that flew here."

Certain deities on this list, and a few who do not appear on it, figure prominently in Chinese folk religion as it survives in Taiwan today. When ancestors of the Taiwanese crossed the Formosa Straits in large numbers during the seventeenth century, they brought their gods with them. Some are simply called kings, deified scholar-officials or government ministers of the past who in their deified form protect against pestilence or dangers at sea. A warrior-type protector, known earlier as "Truly Military Great Emperor," now bears the striking name of "Emperor on High of the Dark Quarter," or "Protecting Holy True Lord of the North Pole Star." The "Great Emperor Who Preserves Life" is known in Taiwan as one who heals the sick.

Two deities very close to the common life of very ordinary people are the god of wealth and the kitchen god. Ts'ai Shen does just what his name implies: he gives wealth and most people have no hesitation about asking him to prosper their endeavors with extra profit. Tzau Wang, the god of the hearth, presides over the kitchen where he receives more or less routine notice day by day. On Chinese New Year's Eve, however, the kitchen god receives special treatment. He is sent up to heaven to report on the family's activities during the preceding year, but many offerings of wine are placed before him before he leaves. If he is a bit befuddled from having imbibed too much, he is likely to forget the more unpleasant happenings and his report will be more impressive.

Shrines to the earth god can be found all over Taiwan: a small hut at the corner of a farmer's field or an image on the floor under a home altar. The earth god, who personifies the spirits of earth and grain worshipped by ancient Chinese, still is believed to bring good crops and prosper the farmer's family.

As this discussion of deities indicates, the Chinese people express continuing devotion to Taoist deities such as Yu Huang, the Jade Emperor, and the immortalized Lao Tzu, as well as to various other gods and immortals. For most people Buddhas and Bodhisattvas function as deities, so they may be added to the pantheon of possibilities. No family or community worships all these deities; instead, over the course of time they will focus devotion on a very few, depending on the needs which must be met and the power they believe a god has demonstrated in meeting those needs.

ACTIVITY IN TEMPLE, HOME, AND ON THE STREET

The ways of worshipping these gods follow a recognizable pattern. First of all a temple is arranged so that one enters an enclosure and finds just about everything needed. Smaller shrines including an ancestral shrine form a wall around the courtyard. There will be a shop selling joss sticks, paper money, and so on, and the shopkeeper is usually a functionary who can tell fortunes and interpret various signs and symbols. Directly in line with the entrance is an altar, or in the case of a large temple a series of altars, pointing toward a central shrine with the main images, whether Buddhas and Bodhisattvas, Taoist deities, Kuan Kung, Matzu, or whatever. Smaller images may be upon the altar just before the central shrine, or on side altars to right and left. Between the various altars or outside the temple enclosure are large receptacles filled with sand where glowing joss sticks may be placed after one has made an offering and bowed with them.

In any one temple there are several possibilities. Worshippers may focus their devotion directly to the god or Buddha in the central shrine or on a side shrine or to all of them. A new temple erected in the sixties in Taipei has Kuan Kung above the central altar, an image and altar to Confucius (most unusual) on the right, and one to Kuan Yin on the left. Up the stairway to a small shrine above there is an image of Lao Tzu. In this temple, as well as in almost every one I visited, there is a shrine in which ancestral plaques have been placed by families living in the vicinity of that temple. They might come and express devotion to ancestors alone, or they might also make offerings to the Buddhas and deities of that temple.

Let us assume, for example, that Mrs. Wang decides to come to this temple on a certain day. It may be the birthday of the god of the temple or the anniversary of the death of one of her relatives. Her husband may be ill or unemployed. She and her husband may want a child, but she is still not pregnant and hopes to become so. She may be pregnant and concerned about the birth of the child. She may have several children, one of whom is ill or facing a big exam. Any of these or countless other reasons may have brought her here. As has been indicated previously, the problem or crisis situation she faces may in large measure determine her choice of a temple. Childbearing concerns, for example, will bring her to the temple of a deity who is believed to be effective in bringing about pregnancy or easy childbirth.

An image of Matzu. The box below the altar is for
offerings to the goddess.

Mrs. Wang enters the large enclosure, places her offering—possibly a bunch of bananas or a chicken—on the first altar, and purchases paper money to burn for her ancestors and joss sticks for her own devotions. Lighting the joss sticks she approaches one of the altar tables and, holding the sticks in both hands in front of her, proceeds to bow from the waist several times while she moves or shakes the joss sticks which by now send forth the fragile fragrance of the incense. She then places the joss sticks in the urn and bows some more. If there is some question about the future of the child, marriage, business, or illness, Mrs. Wang may pick up the divining blocks on the altar and cast them to the floor in the hope of getting an answer to her question. She may of course stop by the ancestral shrine if the tablets to her relatives are enshrined there, light joss sticks in their honor, and burn paper money to care for them. Then Mrs. Wang leaves, presumably comforted or encouraged or inspired, and returns to her normal tasks.

The same flexibility prevails for a shrine at home. The main room of a house, at the center in the traditional U-shaped large family dwelling, is both a shrine and a "living room." The altar table is placed along the wall facing the front door. On the wall in back of the table is a picture or image of the deity worshipped by this family. As with the folk religious temple, it may be a Buddha or Bodhisattva, a Taoist deity, Kuan Kung, Matzu, the god of wealth, or some other. On either side of the picture or image are ancestral plaques to the members of the family, often with photographs of certain persons. Some families may have only the ancestral tablets and photographs and no image of deity or Buddha. Over a long period of time the deity or Buddha worshipped by a family may change, depending on how a particular deity has prospered the family.

On the table itself are candles, usually two, often electric lights in the shape of candles. Three wine cups are placed across the altar for offerings of wine. There may be a basket of flowers, a bowl of fruit, and a small urn for joss sticks. Worship before this altar follows the rhythm of the family and community: seasons of planting and harvesting, anniversaries, times of crisis, holidays, and the feelings of the people. Regardless of how pious or nonchalant a particular family might be, as they come and go they see this reminder of other powers and their relation to everyday concerns.

A folk religious temple plays a major role in community affairs. The celebration of a god's birthday, as seen in the Prologue, involves not only the people who regularly frequent that temple to worship that god but the whole community, often attracting people from neighboring villages and even far distant places. An inescapable feeling of solidarity emerges and, over a period of time, results in lasting social cohesion.

Folk religious activity, both the major festivals and the more humdrum day-to-day devotion of families and individuals in temples or at home, provides a major stimulus to the economic life of a community. Great sums of money must be spent in order to celebrate a festival. Floats are built, new costumes made or old ones repaired, the temple refurbished, musicians and special priests employed. Visitors from out of town either eat in restaurants or are invited to eat with town families, so great quantities of food and drink must be bought, prepared, and served. Practically every woman pays a visit to the beauty parlor and every man goes to the barber shop. It is hard to think of any business or profession which does not benefit. Even the doctors take in more because of many cases of stomach trouble and just plain exhaustion.

Between the several festivals that occur in the course of a year, people must purchase joss sticks, paper money, and various paper objects for home and temple devotion. There are shops which specialize in this business where one can even see many of these articles being made. There are also "god-shops" where images are made by rather expert craftsmen. People can order a Buddha or Kuan Yin or Kuan Kung or earth god or whatever they like.

The political influence of the folk religious temple is a bit more difficult to describe but must not be ignored. As previously mentioned, various Taoist sects have at certain times in history actually raised armies and attacked government centers and troops. Nothing so serious has occurred in a long time, but at the local level political groups associate with certain temples to the extent that one temple functions as the headquarters for one mayoral candidate and another temple functions as the headquarters for another candidate. Supporters of Mr. Chen contribute to the repair and redecoration of a Kuan Kung temple and point to their project as testimony to the honesty and integrity of Mr. Chen. Not to be outdone, the supporters of Mr. Lao do a similar refurbishing job on a Matzu temple which was getting a little run down, and the election fever mounts in intensity. It is impossible to say how many people really look upon such activity as a sign of religious devotion. Most people undoubtedly recognize that both Mr. Chen and Mr. Lao are out for votes. It is hard in any culture for an atheist to be a politician. Given the way in which folk religion penetrates every aspect of Chinese culture, the political realm cannot be immune from religious influence, and religious life is in turn influenced by the political.

In many Chinese communities the temple has served as a school or as a center for distribution of relief supplies. Wanderers have found a place to sleep and a little food to eat in a temple or a Buddhist monastery. Community meetings are held there, and on occasion the appointment of officials is determined by some form of divination. In modern times when a whole village is to be inoculated against a disease, the temple often serves as an inoculation center. Even when government takes over many of these functions, the temple may still be the only place for rest at the noon hour.

Although people who are caught up in the folk religious stream may turn to Confucian, Taoist, or Buddhist literature for guidance, there are other sources. Chinese novels and storybooks usually have a moral in them and may well reflect a religious atmosphere. Traveling bands of actors perform morality plays similar in tone to the morality plays of medieval Europe. In addition, however, there are countless tracts, pamphlets, and booklets which give all kinds of advice on religious matters. For example, *The Silent Way of Recompense* supposedly gives the words of a Taoist deity, Wen Ch'ang, who says:

> For seventeen generations I have been incarnated as a high official, and I have never oppressed the people or my subordinates. I have saved people from misfortune, helped people in need, shown pity to orphans, and forgiven people's mistakes. . . . If you can set your minds on things as I have set mine, Heaven will surely bestow blessings upon you.[2]

Note the reference to incarnation, to compassion, and to the idea of doing certain things in order to gain blessings.

Now see if you can trace the following maxims to Confucian, Taoist, or Buddhist influence, or to the ancient pattern of filial piety.

A woman choosing a joss stick. These sticks of incense can also be used for divination.

Be loyal to your ruler and filial to your parents.

Be respectful toward elders and truthful to friends.

Write and publish holy scriptures and tracts. Build and repair temples and shrines.

Buy captive creatures and set them free, or hold fast to vegetarianism and abstain from taking life.

Do not go into the mountain to catch birds in nets, nor to the water to poison fish and shrimps.

Do not . . . create disharmony between brothers. Do not. . . cause father and son to quarrel.

Always conceal people's vices but proclaim their virtue. Do not say "yes" with your mouth and "no" in your heart.

Follow the principle of Heaven in your work. Obey the dictates of the human heart in your words.

Refrain from doing any evil, but earnestly do all good deeds.

Then there will never be any influence of evil stars upon you but you will always be protected by good and auspicious spirits.

Immediate rewards will come to your own person, and later rewards will reach your posterity.[3]

You should be able to isolate a few passages which speak of virtues in a way that is definitely Confucian. Buddhist influence may be seen in those which speak of compassion for living creatures. Many of them, however, are a mixture of several streams of Chinese religious life and thought, which suggests yet another expression of true Chinese folk religion.

Folk religion, popular religion, or a "people's" religion—whatever term is used—is a combination of component parts, a "mix" of belief and practice. The mixture follows no rhyme or reason except that it makes sense to the people who do the mixing. They believe it works: a god who can get things done responds to their faith and devotion, their rituals and moral actions, in such a way that life seems to go on a little better and future hopes are a bit stronger. If there are no recognizable results, or if the results do not satisfy, then another combination which will bring satisfaction and hope is worked out.

The prevailing combination for a family or a community may have a Confucian character, a Taoist flavor, or Buddhist tendencies, or it may defy any such designation. Nevertheless, the pattern of religious life and thought in that family or community will be sufficiently unified to hold the people together and diverse enough to allow the variety which is the spice of life.

Chapter 6

The Stream Flows On

An ancient main stream of offerings to heaven, earth, and ancestors has received Confucian, Taoist, and Buddhist currents, resulting in a folk religion which allows great variety and flexibility. After absorbing so many different patterns of belief and practice, one would think Chinese religion could absorb anything, but Islam and Christianity never really became a part of the main stream.

Islam has been in China since the seventh century A.D. and claimed fifty million followers at one time, but the majority of Muslims in China have come from minority racial and linguistic groups rather than the Chinese people as such. Muslims in China never adopted typically Chinese religious practices, and the Islamic belief in one God who must not be depicted in any form could never be brought into the main stream of Chinese religion.

Christianity made several appearances in China, beginning as early as the seventh century A.D., and was an extremely influential movement in the first half of the twentieth century. Catholics and Protestants together never numbered more than one percent of the population, however, and even this small number had little to do with indigenous Chinese religious life. Jesuit missionaries in the seventeenth century proposed that Catholics regard the worship of ancestors as a civil ceremony so that it would not conflict with regular Catholic worship. Catholic officialdom did not approve, however, and Christianity has continued as a "foreign religion" in the minds of most Chinese. In recent years both Catholic and Protestant leaders in the Chinese world have explored the possibility of deeper relationships with Chinese religious movements, but it is hard to imagine Christianity adapting to Chinese religion the way Buddhism did.

From the midnineteenth century to the present time Christian leaders have had to deal with the problem of their identification with Europe and the United States. The Western powers with their superior firepower and ships both embarrassed and humiliated the Chinese in a series of incidents. As the last of China's dynasties crumbled in decay, some Chinese leaders read the signs of the times and decided to turn to the West for technology, patterns of government, and even for new values.

In 1911 the Nationalist Revolution toppled the Ch'ing dynasty, and after several power struggles the Republic of China emerged as a basically democratic state. There were no more emperors so there were no more sacrifices to Heaven, for the emperor was the one responsible before Heaven. Full-scale worship of Confucius had been inaugurated in 1905 to shore up the old order; when the old system collapsed, the worship of Confucius went with it. Furthermore, the examination system based on the Confucian Four Books, which one had to pass in order to enter government service, was abolished.

Only eight years after the revolution, on May 4, 1919, university students and teachers broke into the streets and gathered before government offices in Peking to protest the way Chinese officials had allowed China to be mistreated in the peace negotiations after World War I. The Versailles Peace Conference had assigned Germany's former landholdings in China to Japan, and China's representatives had acquiesced. This protest demonstration by students and professors, known as the May Fourth Movement, also called for the use of the colloquial instead of the classical language for literature. The protestors sought to break from the old culture; they questioned filial piety, belief in gods and spirits, and all related practices classified as "superstition." Therefore their banners proclaimed: "Down with the old curiosity shop of Confucius!"

The new generation believed in evolution and scientific testing as devotedly as their ancestors had believed in Buddhas or filial piety. Belief in old ideas eroded further because some students and teachers, including an assistant librarian at Peking University named Mao Tsetung, excited by the Russian Revolution of 1917, began to study Marx and Engels and organized the Communist Party in 1921.

The intellectuals who led the main movements in China during the first half of the twentieth century had little use for religion. Offerings to the earth god and to ancestors were left for peasants, as were practices of divination and geomancy. The *I Ching*, along with Buddhist and Taoist literature, was scorned by college graduates as being beneath their dignity. Therefore most of the people who could talk to foreigners said religion was an affair for the ignorant masses and would die out with education and modernization.

The interpreters who drew such conclusions did not know the peasant masses very well. In spite of all that has happened, both sides of filial piety—obedience to the living elders and proper rites in honor of the dead—have continued to the present day. The new intellectuals allow their children much more freedom, but respect for parents is still expected. People still sweep the graves, burn paper money, and offer food and wine to their ancestors as they did in the ancient past. The festivals of spring and autumn, when such ancestral rites hit their peak, are observed in an urban center of trade and industry like Hong Kong, as well as in the more traditional centers in Southeast Asia and Taiwan. The People's Republic of China is a different story, reserved for the end of this chapter.

Shrines to T'u Ti Kung, the earth god, can be found in the corner of almost every Chinese farmer's field, and there are signs that joss sticks have been placed in the small urn or tin can in front of the image. There are communities in Taiwan where T'u Ti Kung is the chief deity; a huge image of him towers over the cemetery across the road from the university where I taught in Taiwan.

Divination by several methods continues, although the *I Ching* seems to be more popular in the West than it does in Asia at the moment. The heating of tortoise shells died out thousands of years ago, but the divining blocks can be heard banging against the floor at any time of the day in any temple. The *feng shui* artist or geomancer still selects sites for buildings and graves; Western businessmen and missionaries can cause great hostility if they erect buildings that disturb what local people believe the *feng shui* to be.

Confucius' teaching with its religious dimensions has also survived the scornful attacks of the earlier part of this century. The values of righteousness, propriety, reciprocity, and loyalty—which combine to mean humanity, wisdom, and sincerity—are extolled and exemplified by many Chinese people today. Children repeat his maxims in school. Confucius' words about spirits have been interpreted by the scholar class to mean that he really did not believe in spirits, but the common people still worship the spirits without any feeling of going against Confucius. Significantly, when President Chiang Kai-shek devised his New Life Movement to counter liberal ideas in 1933, he chose several Confucian virtues—propriety, righteousness, integrity, and the sense of shame—as an ideology for the movement which his followers still promote today.

Confucius' birthday, celebrated in a September predawn ceremony in at least three cities in Taiwan, is ostensibly a civil, cultural ceremony, but it symbolizes deep reserves of meaning. Young boys in ancient costumes perform with great precision a series of dances which go back as far as the T'ang dynasty. Officials of the cities in which the ceremony takes place are dressed in traditional Chinese attire and are very proper as they go through more sedate movements. Young people in school uniforms are required to attend, but a surprisingly large number of average people show up. An air of solemn mystery gives way to happy excitement as everyone tries to pull some bristles from a giant boar which has been killed and roasted. Ancient culture is still transmitted at the birthday of the Great Transmitter.

In 1958 several refugee scholars who belong to the Neo-Confucian school of philosophy issued a "Manifesto to the World in Behalf of Chinese Culture," in which they emphatically affirmed belief in a profound spiritual element in Chinese culture. They went on to say that this spiritual element has a transcendent quality that is necessary if "harmony is to prevail between heaven and earth and man as described in the ancient classics."[1] Chinese people are very practical, these scholars admitted, but practical life is preserved and protected by a mood which goes beyond the practical. Two young Chinese scholars, now living and teaching in the United States, have also spoken of the transcendent element in Confucian thought, thus altering the trend established by young intellectuals in the earlier part of this century.

What of Taoism? When I first began to study the religions of Asia in the years following World War II, I heard that Taoist philosophy had meaning for only a few old-timers and that Taoist religion was dying out even among the "ignorant masses." What an amazing surprise it is to discover that intellectuals in East and West are saying that Taoist philosophy has something to say to the modern world and that Taoist priests continue their ancient rituals with a devotion and precision which would put many a priesthood to shame.

A Taoist festival like the one described in Chapter 3 took place in the fall of 1972 in northern Taiwan. Several young Americans were privileged to observe the ceremony and have witnessed similar ones in other parts of Taiwan. A tape recording and slides taken of this event reveal that the priests who recited the liturgy entered sincerely into the celebration. It was indeed a time of renewal and new life for priests and people.

Christopher Schipper, a European scholar, relates that several years ago he went to Taiwan to study Taoist texts in a research library. He found his way, however, into a Taoist community in the southern part of the island where he discovered

> that the liturgy still employed by the Taoist priest in Taiwan is very much the same as the one we have in obscure and fragmentary form, in the Tao Tsang [voluminous Taoist scripture]. . . . The fact that the same liturgy prevails all over shows us for the first time that there must have been, at least for the last 1500 years, a kind of common Taoist liturgy for all China.[2]

Professor Schipper also discovered that both the rare ordained priest and the common unordained, or lay, priest trace their succession back to China for something like forty generations. The memorizing of rituals, about a hundred in all, along with training in dancing, music, and acrobatics, all begin at a very early age. The ordained or chief priest must demonstrate agility and strength, as well as powers of concentration and outstanding personal qualities.

Ancient philosophical ideas are still alive. The interaction of *yang* and *yin* is emphasized in Taoism and is symbolized in many of its rites. Newspaper articles in Taiwan in the late sixties suggested a life of nonstriving, or *wu-wei,* so-called nonaction. An editorial criticized too much government bureaucracy, too many government control measures. This rare complaint about the government quoted Lao Tzu and the Taoist ideal of a minimum of government control. Taoism may not be as obvious as Confucianism, but it lives on just the same.

The Buddhist current is more obvious than either Confucianism or Taoism. In Hong Kong, Taiwan, and the Chinese communities of Southeast Asia, large crowds attend ceremonies celebrating the birthday of the Buddha as well as his "ascension to heaven." Devoted Buddhists hold "let live" ceremonies as described in Chapter 4, in which fish or birds are released following the precept which forbids taking life.

Buddhist monks and nuns are a fairly common sight in Taiwan. Men and women are still being ordained, as in late 1966 when a mass ordination ceremony was held for 336 nuns and 91 monks. There are also formal rites for receiving men and women as lay followers of the Buddha. Chinese monks do not go about on daily begging rounds as do their counterparts in Southeast Asia, but as winter approaches monks and nuns make a tour of the streets and receive cash donations and clothing for the winter months ahead. Taiwanese monks tend to marry and have families, following the example of Japanese monks.

As was the case in the T'ang dynasty and through the centuries, Buddhists engage in educational and charitable work, thus expressing the compassion of the Bodhisattva. The China Buddhist Association in Taiwan sponsors clinics at which doctors provide services free of charge. Buddhists in Hong Kong opened a 350-bed hospital in 1970 with a ceremony and an international seminar on healing and social work. They have a fine record in establishing schools in Hong Kong. A Buddhist seminary was opened in southern Taiwan in the late sixties and a Buddhist research center is at work in the north.

T'ai Hsu, a monk who initiated several reform projects in China in the first half of this century is memorialized with a literature center in

Taipei. This monk, who was concerned about the education and discipline of his fellow monks and about Buddhism's intellectual appeal to the modern world, inspired a number of monks and laymen who work today in Hong Kong, Taiwan, and Southeast Asia.

Buddhists in the Chinese world are not at all shy in witnessing to their faith. In the early sixties a giant Buddha image was constructed on a hilltop outside the city of Changhua in central Taiwan. Large crowds continue to come to view the image which is taller than the famous Great Buddha in Kamakura, Japan. Not to be outdone, Buddhists in Taichung, another city in central Taiwan, constructed another Buddha image which they claim is taller than either of the others. Unfortunately this latest image is on level ground and therefore does not look as tall.

I went to the dedication of a new Buddhist temple in Taichung in early 1971. An older temple stood across the street and crowds of people moved back and forth between the new and the old. The new temple was dedicated to Kuan Yin, the Bodhisattva who hears the cries of the world. Inside the building there is not only her image, but 3,333 small niches, each containing a small Buddha image which could serve as an ancestral plaque. Some already had the names of Buddhist faithful inscribed in them.

A prominent Buddhist leader and scholar came from the capital city, along with another monk who was hailed as a living Buddha. There was an impressive ceremony in which a woman who headed a lay women's organization cut the ribbon and people poured into the new temple where the ceremonies continued.

Outside the new temple were numerous life-size images of animals. The sculpture was very poor, but the children who gathered around the

The giant Buddha image at Changhua, Taiwan.

72

images were quite impressed. An ingenious program planner staged an art contest in which the children were set to work sketching the animals in the hope of getting a prize. There was something for everyone, even for people willing to share with a foreigner their joy in the occasion.

Most visible of all is Chinese folk religion which unites all the currents considered in this book into a continuing stream. Wherever I went in Taiwan I could see old temples being repaired and new ones being constructed. Temples themselves are not so obvious in other parts of the Chinese world, but they are everywhere in Taiwan.

One doesn't live in a Chinese community long before he hears the word *pai-pai,* which is pronounced like "bye-bye" in English. People are not saying good-bye but are referring to a religious festival which involves a whole community or countryside in a celebration of the god's birthday. The Matzu festival described at the beginning of this book was such an occasion, featuring parades, floats, music, dancing, magic, offerings in the temple and at other shrines, and carrying the god through the streets in a palanquin.

Although a *pai-pai* is the most striking expression of the vitality of folk religion in Taiwan, one may see other signs of a religion in which many people participate. Funerals with Western and Chinese bands, acrobats, floats, mourners, and priests provide evidence of the interrelation of folk religion and the common life. Fortune-tellers, physiognomists, and geomancers all ply their trade. There are shops which sell religious articles. At least every other shop along a city street, regardless of the business, will have its small shrine or god shelf, with the glowing joss sticks to indicate recent use. In neighborhood districts almost every home will have some sort of altar or god shelf holding an image of Kuan Yin, Matzu, or some other deity.

Many observers question whether religion in the Chinese world can survive industrialization, modernization, and the increasing secularization of modern life. Young people certainly do not participate in religious activities as frequently or as fully as their parents and grandparents did. Those who go to college usually appear scornful of what they call superstition, although one gets the impression that expressing this attitude is "the thing to do" among college students.

A Chinese scholar who wrote his doctoral thesis on folk religion in his native Taiwan says that the ancestral tradition helps people maintain "the continuity of tradition and an eternal chain of life by identifying . . . with the ancestors."[3] By making offerings to the spirits, people have a feeling of participating in ongoing dynamic life and in the total cosmos. The people have a feeling of spiritual enrichment and receive further a sense of common identity with the land, their ancestors, and the community. This holds true not only for elderly people, but for younger people as well. For some people in the Chinese world, religion is a vital part of their lives.

All of these examples of contemporary Chinese religious life have come from Taiwan, Hong Kong, and the Chinese communities of Southeast Asia. Only about 3 percent of the Chinese live in those places, however, whereas about 96 percent live in the People's Republic of China. To what extent does religion of any sort survive among the vast majority of the Chinese?

There is no evidence to suggest the large-scale religious activity in China that one finds in Taiwan. On the contrary, any public or institutional expression of religion in China itself is so minimal as to be imperceptible. Most of the temples, monasteries, mosques, and churches have either been closed or turned into schools, granaries, storage facilities, or living quarters. Celebrations of the Buddha's birthday, Christmas and Easter, and the beginning and end of the Muslim month of fasting, called Ramadan, were reported until the mid-sixties, but only the Muslim celebrations received public notice in the early seventies. The spring festival, when graves are visited and swept, receives minimal observance. There is slight evidence that here and there a temple, mosque, or church was reopened in the mid-seventies, but the number of people worshipping in any one place is infinitesimally small.

Within two years after the establishment of the People's Republic of China in 1949, the government pressed for the formation of associations which would communicate government decisions and programs to religious groups and relay responses and reactions by the groups to the government. The first to appear was a Protestant organization, the Three-Self Movement, which was to focus on self-support, self-administration, and self-propagation. The Chinese Buddhist and Chinese Muslim Associations were soon formed; the Taoist Association was organized much later. Catholics strongly resisted the National Catholic Patriotic Association but finally gave in. The name of the last-mentioned indicates an element that was true for all: these groups were intended to rally support for the government.

Criticism of religion by officials and the masses mounted sharply in spite of official organizations. Confucius was criticized several times as a reactionary, feudal philosopher. One contemporary Marxist thinker wrote a book in which he referred to Confucius' method of "self-cultivation" which Communist cadres might emulate. Although he was careful to disavow any Confucian content, he was criticized severely in later years for harboring feudal thoughts.

Taoists and Buddhists have been attacked for superstitious practices and for their vague philosophies of emptiness which divert people from the world of work. As in the T'ang dynasty, monks and nuns have had to leave the cloister and join labor groups. Taoist secret societies were difficult to discover and root out, but the government was finally successful in doing so. These movements which were clearly Chinese in character at least did not have the disadvantage of being called the "running dog of foreign imperialists," a label pinned on Christian groups, but it was hard going for all.

Folk religion has turned out to be the most effective in surviving in a state not friendly to religion. There was no way to organize a "Chinese Folk Religion Association." Little ancestral shrines, temples to the Queen of Heaven (like Matzu), altars to Kuan Kung or T'u Ti Kung were everywhere. If a zealous work team tears one down or stores grain in it, the villagers can turn elsewhere. They themselves can take down the shrines when antireligious campaigns are severe and put it up again when the tide changes. Push folk religion down in one village and it pops up again later somewhere else. People who follow a folk religion know how to give and take in order to survive.

The People's Republic of China adopted a constitution which included a provision allowing freedom of religious belief, which of course would allow freedom not to believe in religion. This provision was interpreted to mean that religion could be practiced only within the walls of temples and churches but not outside such religious buildings, so as not to interfere with social and political activities. The freedom not to believe was given steady publicity by articles in newspapers and magazines in which religion and superstition were equated. The standard Marxist criticisms of religion were stated: religion is the opiate of the people, a tool used by capitalists and imperialists to lull people into submission so they will not revolt, and a distraction from the big tasks of social reconstruction.

The last point designates the trend which prevailed. The attention and loyalty of the people young and old were directed to the building of a new society. Economic production, whether on farm or in factory, became the all-consuming passion. Everyone had to examine himself and be criticized by his comrades as to political correctness. If there appears to be a fault (or sin), one must confess and keep confessing until he really gets it right. People must develop class consciousness and then struggle against the upper classes.

Individuals, families, work teams, students, soldiers, artists—all were summoned to build the new China. Religion was seen to be part of the past along with the glorious art and architecture. New China's focus turned to the present tasks and struggles to carry the revolution through to the end, the revolution which had cut off the past.

Some Western interpreters of the China scene maintain that the devotion expended by at least the leaders in revolutionary China is akin to religious devotion. Given the Marxist critique of religion, this seems a strange thing to say. Any Chinese Communist vigorously denies that his commitment to lifelong struggle has anything to do with religion.

For Marxists there is no god, but the revolutionary process, what Marxists call the dialectic of history, functions as a powerful reality that evokes their ultimate concern. This must be carried through to the end. Songs and dances and drama can be seen as the liturgical expression of one's commitment to the revolutionary process. The moral element is also very strong, for Chinese Communists are expected to live simply, waste nothing, and be scrupulously honest and forthright. The "faithful" are grouped together in the Communist Party, or in the Young Communist League, or various other auxiliaries which give a strong sense of group solidarity. Everyone joins in the celebrations of the October 1, 1949, founding of the People's Republic, "Love the People Month," Women's Day, and so on through the calendar.

Religion in China may be viewed another way. In Chinese folk religion a deified hero receives the devotion of the people because he was effective in his lifetime and proves effective in later years when people turn to him for help. The revolution accomplished something and people are proud that China once again must be respected as a powerful nation. The leader Mao Tse-tung, who died in 1976, symbolizes the feat of "getting things done"; therefore he and his thought are enshrined, the deified hero with his bible. He is the ultimate deified hero. Thus a basic motif in Chinese folk religion is invested with new meaning and the process goes on: Kuan Kung in the past, Mao today, someone else tomorrow. China's fluid folk religion continues to move forward as a stream with many currents, for it has the capacity to absorb and transform a seemingly endless variety of beliefs and practices, gods and heroes, as they come and go.

Notes

Chapter 1: The Source of the Stream in Ancient Times

1. James Legge, trans., *Sacred Books of the East,* Vol. III (Oxford: Clarendon Press, 1899), p. 388.

2. Ibid., pp. 352–53.

3. *The I Ching or Book of Changes,* 3d ed. of the Richard Wilhelm translation rendered into English by Cary F. Baynes (Princeton, N.J.: Princeton University Press, 1967), pp. 48–49.

4. Ibid., pp. 50–52.

5. Legge, *Sacred Books of the East,* Vol. III, p. 488.

Chapter 2: The Confucian Current

1. *Analects* 7:1, in Wing-tsit Chan, ed., *A Source Book in Chinese Philosophy* (Princeton, N.J.: Princeton University Press, 1963), p. 31. Subsequent quotations from the *Analects* are from this volume and are designated by traditional chapter and verse in parentheses following each quotation.

2. Chan, *A Source Book in Chinese Philosophy,* p. 55.

3. Ibid., pp. 57–58.

4. Ibid., p. 214.

5. Lin Yutang, ed. and trans., *The Wisdom of Confucius* (New York: The Modern Library, 1938), pp. 114–15.

Chapter 3: The Taoist Current

1. Chan, *A Source Book in Chinese Philosophy,* p. 190.

2. Ibid., p. 209.

3. Michael Saso, *Taoism and the Rite of Cosmic Renewal* (Pullman, Wash.: Washington State University Press, 1972), pp. 38–44.

Chapter 4: The Character of Buddhism in China

1. Kenneth Ch'en, *Buddhism in China* (Princeton, N.J.: Princeton University Press, 1964), p. 296.

2. Ibid., p. 232.

3. Both verses are from Chan, *A Source Book in Chinese Philosophy,* pp. 431–32.

4. D. T. Suzuki, *Essays in Zen Buddhism,* First Series (London: Luzac and Company, 1927), p. 163.

Chapter 5: Popular Folk Religion

1. C. K. Yang, *Religion in Chinese Society* (Berkeley: University of California Press, 1961), pp. 7–15.

2. William T. de Bary, ed., *Sources of Chinese Tradition* (New York: Columbia University Press, 1960), p. 635.

3. Ibid., pp. 636–37.

Chapter 6: The Stream Flows On

1. Translated by Robert P. Kramers in *Quarterly Notes on Christianity and Chinese Religion,* Vol. II, No. 2 (May, 1958), pp. 1–25.

2. Christopher Schipper, "Priest and Liturgy" (mimeographed).

3. Chiu Ming-chung, "Two Types of Folk Piety: . . . Folk Religions in Formosa" (Dissertation, University of Chicago, 1970), p. 107.

Glossary

Bodhisattva. One who has attained *bodhi,* or enlightenment, but postpones Nirvana in order to help others. Functions as a saving saint in Mahayana Buddhism.

Buddha. One who has attained *bodhi,* or enlightenment, and has entered Nirvana.

divination. The art and practice of foretelling future events or determining a course of action by studying the stars, flight pattern of birds, or other activities.

diviner. One who practices divination.

feng shui. The Chinese name for geomancy, a branch of divination employed to determine appropriate sites for houses or graves. Literally translated as "wind-water."

Five Classics. Five ancient Chinese books: *Book of Poetry (Shih Ching), Book of Rites (Li Chi), Book of History (Shu Ching), Book of Changes (I Ching), Spring and Autumn Annals (Ch'un Ch'iu).* The Five Classics and the Four Books are the authoritative works on Chinese culture, especially for Confucian scholars.

Four Books. The *Analects, Book of Mencius, Doctrine of the Mean,* and *Great Learning.* With the Five Classics, they comprise the authoritative canon on Chinese culture according to the Confucian tradition.

Hinduism. The beliefs, practices, and socio-cultural relationships which make up the dominant religion of India. The ultimate divine reality is known through a host of deities which people may approach in many ways to gain the goods of life and union with the divine.

iconography. Images, figures, or pictures intended to represent personalities or deities important to a religion.

Jainism. An ascetic religious movement which originated in India about the same time (sixth century B.C.) as Buddhism, emphasizing ascetic practices, nonviolence, and protection of all forms of life.

Lotus Sutra. Probably the most popular Buddhist text in China and Japan. A great assembly of Buddhas and Bodhisattvas hears the message that all beings will be saved and become Buddhas.

Mahayana. The form of Buddhism prevalent in China, Japan, Korea, and Vietnam. Literally translated as "great vehicle."

Mandate of Heaven. Authorization of power to Chinese kings and emperors believed traditionally to issue from Heaven.

Mithra(s). An Iranian god of light who became the center of a mystery cult which spread to the Mediterranean world, China, and other places.

Nestorian Christians. A branch of the Christian church which began in the fifth century and emphasized the complete and authentic union of divine and human in Jesus Christ, rather than the swallowing up of the human into the divine.

Nirvana. Literally a "snuffing out" or "extinction" of the flames of desire or craving, but regarded positively as an indescribable yet blissful state which is the ultimate goal in Buddhism.

Pure Land school. A Chinese and Japanese denomination or branch of Buddhism emphasizing faith in the Buddha Amitabha which brings rebirth in a heaven called Pure Land or Western Paradise.

sangha. The Buddhist monastic order or community which affirms strict vows and is committed to meditation and service.

Shingon. An esoteric Buddhist school of life and thought which died out in China, where it was known as Chen Yen (True Word), but survives as one of the more important schools or denominations in Japan.

sutra. A Buddhist text or scripture which is regarded as a discourse of the Buddha or derived directly from his teaching.

White Lotus Society. A Chinese Buddhist group which began in the twelfth century and emphasized vegetarianism, repentance, and suppression of desires, plus defense against barbarian invaders.

yang, yin. Complementary and interacting forces of nature such as light and dark, aggressive and passive, male and female.

Zoroastrianism. The religion of ancient Persia which is based on a dualistic theology that depicts a god of goodness and light in continuing struggle with a deity of darkness and evil.

Bibliography

The following works have been selected because (1) they are available for purchase, usually in both hardback and paperback, (2) they contribute in some measure to the understanding of religion in China, and (3) they may be used either by instructors for background reading or by students for reading assignments.

Ahern, Emily M. *The Cult of the Dead in a Chinese Village.* Stanford: Stanford University Press, 1973. An anthropological study of the role of the ancestral cult in a present-day village in northern Taiwan.

Bush, Richard C. *Religion in Communist China.* Nashville, Tenn.: Abingdon Press, 1970. Basically a gathering of available information about religious developments during the first twenty years of the People's Republic of China. In spite of inaccuracies, it remains the only treatment of what has happened to all the major religious movements since 1949.

Chan Wing-tsit. *Religious Trends in Modern China.* New York: Octagon Books, 1969. (Originally published by Columbia University Press, 1953) Although Chan deals more with philosophy than religion, this is the best book on religion in China during the first half of the twentieth century.

————, ed. *A Sourcebook in Chinese Philosophy.* Princeton: Princeton University Press, 1963. Although the selections are chosen for their significance in Chinese philosophy, many are tremendously important for religion.

Ch'en, Kenneth. *Buddhism in China: A Historical Survey.* Princeton: Princeton University Press, 1972. A first-class study of the nature and character of Buddhism from its rise in China to the early years of the People's Republic.

De Bary, William T., ed. *Sources of Chinese Tradition.* 2 vols. New York: Columbia University Press, 1960. The documents collected depict many facets of Chinese culture, with religious dimensions apparent at almost every point.

Fung Yu-lan, *A Short History of Chinese Philosophy.* abr. ed. Edited by Derk Bodde. New York: Free Press, 1966. If study of religion should lead one to philosophy, this book with Chan's *Sourcebook* above are the best guides along the way.

Hsu, Francis L. K. *Under the Ancestor's Shadow.* rev. and enl. ed. New York: Doubleday Anchor Books, 1967. (Originally published by Columbia University Press, 1948) The result of Hsu's field work in western China about 1942, this anthropological study is a classic work on the mainstream of Chinese religion, the ancestral tradition.

Jordan, David K. *Gods, Ghosts, and Ancestors.* Berkeley: University of California Press, 1973. A fascinating study of folk religious life in a rural town in southern Taiwan. Excellent photographs.

MacInnis, Donald E. *Religious Policy and Practice in Communist China.* Edited by Clement Alexandre. New York: Macmillan Co., 1972. A collection of documents primarily illustrating government policy toward religion in general and Christianity in particular. A few selections relate to Buddhism.

Smith, D. Howard. *Chinese Religions.* New York: Holt, Rinehart and Winston, 1971. The best one-volume survey of religion in China. Good photographs.

Thompson, Lawrence G. *Chinese Religion: An Introduction.* 2d ed. Encino, Calif.: Dickenson Publishing Co., 1975. Brief, helpful discussion of main currents in Chinese religion.

————, ed. *The Chinese Way in Religion.* Encino, Calif.: Dickenson Publishing Co., 1973. Good collection of documents on Chinese religion past and present.

Waley, Arthur. *Three Ways of Thought in Ancient China.* New York: Doubleday Anchor Books, 1956. (Originally published by Allen and Unwin [London] 1939) Especially interesting chapters on Chuang-tzu and Mencius.

————, trans. and ed. *The Way and Its Power.* New York: Grove Press, 1958. Still the most beautiful translation of the *Tao Te Ching* in English.

Welch, Holmes. *The Practice of Chinese Buddhism (1900–1950).* Cambridge: Harvard University Press, 1967. Wide-ranging description of Buddhist practice derived from conversations with monks of recent times. (Two later volumes in Welch's series on Chinese Buddhism, although too specialized for this bibliography, should be mentioned: *The Buddhist Revival in China,* 1968, and *Buddhism Under Mao,* 1972.)

————. *Taoism: The Parting of the Way.* Boston: Beacon Press, 1966. Intriguing treatment of Taoist philosophical and religious streams.

Wolf, Arthur P., ed. *Religion and Ritual in Chinese Society.* Stanford: Stanford University Press, 1974. Several perceptive essays on contemporary religious practice.

Wright, Arthur F. *Buddhism in Chinese History.* Stanford: Stanford University Press, 1959. Competent but shorter than Kenneth Ch'en's work.

Yang, C. K. *Religion in Chinese Society.* Berkeley: University of California Press, 1961. The best single work on Chinese folk religion.